The Love That Made
Mother Teresa

David Scott

The Love That Made Mother Teresa

How Her Secret Visions and Dark Nights Can Help You Conquer the Slums of Your Heart

SOPHIA INSTITUTE PRESS
Manchester, New Hampshire

Sophia Institute Press
Box 5284, Manchester, NH 03108
1-800-888-9344

www.SophiaInstitute.com

Sophia Institute Press® is a registered trademark of Sophia Institute.

Library of Congress Cataloging-in-Publication Data

Names: Scott, David, 1961- author.
Title: The love that made Mother Teresa : how her secret visions and dark
   nights can help you conquer the slums of your heart / David Scott.
Other titles: Revolution of love
Description: Manchester, New Hampshire : Sophia Institute Press, 2016. |
   Originally published: 2013. | Includes bibliographical references.
Identifiers: LCCN 2016022605 | ISBN 9781622823628 (pbk. : alk. paper)
Subjects: LCSH: Teresa, Mother, 1910-1997.
Classification: LCC BX4406.5.Z8 S36 2016 | DDC 271/.97—dc23 LC re-
cord available at https://lccn.loc.gov/2016022605

First printing

For Jacob

Contents

Part IV
Mother in Our Dark Time

Foreword

The Church is beautiful in her saints. One of the Church Fathers said that long ago. And it's true.

The saints are living witnesses to Jesus Christ in every age and every culture. They show us what following Christ looks like in "real life" and how to fulfill God's plan for our lives—which is for us to become more like Jesus and become saints ourselves.

As David Scott writes in this fine little book, St. Teresa of Kolkata was probably the most familiar Christian face of our generation. Her works of love, done for the abandoned and forsaken in a remote city in India, made hers a household name the world over.

This book represents something of a new way of writing about the saints. It's part biography, part spiritual reading of our times. There is also a strong apologetic aspect. Scott suggests that Mother Teresa is "God's response" to the signs of our times—a witness to the power and beauty of the gospel message in a world marked by the shadow of death and a growing indifference to God.

Mother Teresa gave up her privileged position and all her possessions to live as one of the world's poor and forgotten and to bring them the light of Christ and the love of God. Her message to the rest of us was direct: we should seek our salvation in the God who comes to us in the poor and the outcast. We should seek Jesus at the margins of society in what she called "his distressing disguise."

The Love That Made Mother Teresa

Always she returned to Jesus' parable of the last judgment: "As you did it to one of the least of these my brethren, you did it to me."

Our Holy Father Pope Francis has said that we should reread often the twenty-fifth chapter of St. Matthew's Gospel, where Jesus identifies himself with the "least of these"—the hungry and the thirsty, the naked and the sick, the prisoner and the immigrant. "If you want to know what you actually have to do," the pope says, "read Matthew Chapter 25, which is the standard by which we will be judged."

Mother Teresa told us the same thing. Again and again, she reminded us that our love for the poor would be the measure of our love for God. We love God as much as we love the most vulnerable and despised among us. What we give to them, we give to him. The love we refuse them is the love we refuse God.

In her life, Mother Teresa did everything for the love of Jesus and the truth of his gospel. She understood that truth without love is cruelty and love without truth is sentimentality. So she spoke the truth in love—through her work with the poor and the dying, through her advocacy for the unborn and the handicapped, through her dedication to peace and justice in the world. And through her witness, we came to see that in God's eyes we are all his beloved sons and daughters and no one should be a stranger to any of us.

As St. Francis did many centuries before, Mother Teresa preached the gospel with her life. And love was the language she used. She understood that love alone is credible in a world where more and more people have drifted from God and live as if he does not exist.

That's why the saints are so important. Because our world will be converted, not by words and programs, but by witnesses. By people who will testify—through the way they live—that Jesus Christ is real and that his gospel has the power to change lives. Our world will be converted only by saints.

Scott's book reminds us, as Mother Teresa always did, that God calls all of us to holiness, to be saints—maybe not saints who

Foreword

are known on the world stage, as Mother Teresa was, but saints of the everyday and missionaries of his love. He calls us to bear witnesses to his love in the ordinary events and activities of our daily lives—in our homes, at school, in the places where we work, going out to meet people wherever they are, even in the shadows and margins of our society.

My prayer is that this book will help us to grow in our appreciation of this amazing woman of God. May we give ourselves to our Blessed Mother Mary, as Mother Teresa did. And may Mother Teresa's life inspire us to love as she loved—making our lives something beautiful that we may offer to God.

Most Reverend José H. Gomez
Archbishop of Los Angeles
December 16, 2013

The Love That Made
Mother Teresa

Part I

The Scent of Sanctity

You know my God.
My God is called love.

Mother Teresa

A Mother Made Blessed

What's so special about Mother Teresa? Why did everybody from the president of the United States to your neighbor next door call her a "living saint"? Why, now that she is dead, is the Roman Catholic Church ready to affirm with finality that she is dwelling in heaven, near to the face of God, a saint from whom we can ask prayers and after whom we can pattern our lives?

If we go with the official definition of a saint from the Catholic catechism, we would say she is worthy of sainthood because she "practiced heroic virtue"—that she lived by faith, hope, and love and was prudent, just, temperate, and brave. St. John Paul II said as much on October 19, 2003, when he beatified Mother Teresa during a solemn ceremony before a throng of three hundred thousand devotees in St. Peter's Square at the Vatican.

In advancing her status from "blessed" to "saint" on September 4, 2016, Pope Francis described her as a living witness to God's mercy. Francis had met Mother Teresa in Rome in 1994, when he was still a cardinal from Buenos Aires. At the time, he joked about how tough she was, saying he would have been afraid of her if she had been his religious superior.

Mother Teresa, in fact, met all four of the popes who have led the Catholic Church since the mid-1960s—and she left her mark on each of them. Not only for her toughness, but for her humble love for Jesus and her selfless service to the poorest of the poor. But force of personality alone does not explain why the Church has inscribed her name in the official canon or register of saints.

Nonetheless, now that Mother Teresa has been canonized as St. Teresa of Kolkata, you can name churches after her, pray for her help, read her writings as bearing a certain divine stamp of approval, and make her your role model. The Church will celebrate her feast day every year on September 5, the anniversary of the day she died in 1997.

None of this, however, helps us figure out what qualifies her for such lofty stature in the first place.

It cannot be because she led a stirring life. She has no dramatic conversion story. She wasn't knocked off a horse and blinded by a brilliant light and a voice from heaven, as St. Paul was. We find with her none of the high sexual drama that Augustine confessed. There is none of the shuttle diplomacy of Bridget of Sweden or Catherine of Siena. Unlike St. Thomas More, she didn't have her head chopped off for standing in the way of a lusty king's ambitions. Her contemporary Padre Pio, declared a saint in 2002, was a stigmatic, one whose hands and feet bore wounds like those of Christ. Teresa wasn't one of those either.

Mother Teresa was simply a cradle Catholic raised in a pious, generous home, who went off at age eighteen to be a nun in the missions in Kolkata, India, which in her lifetime was known as Calcutta. Some years later, she was riding on a train, and she heard a voice that she took to be that of Jesus telling her to leave her religious order to serve the poor. So that's what she did.

But the work that made her famous, while admirable, wasn't all that exceptional, especially for a nun. You can find plenty of people doing what she did — taking care of the sick and the dying, finding homes for abandoned children, defending the poor, the unwanted, and the unborn.

There is no denying she was a devout, deeply prayerful woman who knew her Bible. But a great spiritual master, a poet laureate of the soul — these things she was apparently not. She was a saint of the commonplace — a sound-bite saint — uttering gnomic things such as, "Do something beautiful for God" and "Many people are talking about the poor, but very few people talk to the poor."

"Saints should always be judged guilty until they are proved innocent," the great essayist George Orwell wrote of Mahatma Gandhi. And there have always been plenty of people ready to bring up Mother Teresa on charges of being a great fakir in whom can be found much guile, a kind of Trojan horse for reactionary popery and medieval morals, a peddler of religious Prozac for the poor.

That's not unusual. Saints always attract their share of detractors and devil's advocates. The sermons of St. John Vianney so incensed dance-hall proprietors in his nineteenth-century French town that they used to send ladies of ill repute to sing lewd songs outside his window about how he had sired love-children by them.

A lot of people didn't like what Mother Teresa stood for either. She drew fire from a loose coalition of atheists and agnostics, abortion advocates, and others who wanted the Catholic Church of the late twentieth century to start endorsing a lot of things it had never endorsed before — women priests, birth control, violent revolution, divorce, and more.

What really seemed to rankle her detractors was the success of the religious order she founded, the Missionaries of Charity — more than four thousand nuns serving the poor in 123 countries by the time of her death in 1997, along with another four hundred or so religious "brothers" and thousands of lay volunteers.

What her opponents couldn't explain, some tried to chalk up to corruption and ill-gotten gain. But even these folks couldn't turn any real dirt on her.

One of Orwell's brightest disciples, British journalist Christopher Hitchens, tried the hardest. But his 1995 exposé, *The Missionary Position*, when shorn of its antireligious cant, actually exposed very little: her hospices for the destitute dying needed modernizing;

she kept the names of those who gave her money confidential, along with the amounts of their donations; and she sometimes supped with sinners and accepted contributions from them.

Reality with Mother Teresa was far less sinister: she worked hard, prayed a lot, lived simply, and died as she lived—her personal effects consisting of a prayer book, a pair of sandals, and a couple of saris, the trademark blue and white linen habit of her order.

2

What Becomes a Saint

Is this enough to make you a saint — to lead a simple, prayerful life and do good unto others? Yes and no. Inevitably, with this line of questioning, you wind up taking a sort of reductionist approach to sainthood, as if being named a saint is like getting the gold watch for a lifetime of loyal Catholic service.

To really understand why the Church wants to call Mother Teresa a saint and to understand her meaning for our times requires putting out into the depths of the Catholic psyche and imagination. Other religious traditions esteem holy men and women (mostly men, it must be said): Buddhists have bodhisattvas and Hindus their gurus; Jews have *tzaddikim* and Muslims their *awliya' Allah*. Only in Catholicism do we find holy humans at the center of the cult and culture of the religion, as if hardwired into the deep structures of believers' identities.

"Our Church is the Church of the saints . . . Those who have once realized this have found their way to the very heart of the Catholic faith," Catholic essayist and novelist Georges Bernanos wrote in the 1930s.

The outsider sees only what he labels as kitsch — St. Christopher medals on dashboards, "Thank you, St. Jude!" ads in the classifieds, animal and throat blessings, Madonnas with puppy-dog eyes and flaming hearts. But even these more exuberant expressions of popular piety reflect a sensibility that's authentically and uniquely Catholic.

The Love That Made Mother Teresa

Catholics hold that God, the maker of the universe, came down from heaven and became a real flesh-and-blood man named Jesus; that he grew from an embryo in a mother's womb, experienced all the joys and anguish of human existence, save for sin; that he died and rose, body and soul, into heaven. Catholics believe that this same Jesus every day becomes their real food and drink, that he comes to their altars always and everywhere his Church remembers his death and Resurrection in the Eucharist.

God does all this, Catholics believe, because he wants human beings to share in his very own life. This is the essence of a short prayer the priest prays silently at the altar before every Eucharist: "By the mingling of this water and wine, may we come to share in the divinity of Christ, who humbled himself to share in our humanity."

Think of the saints as God's answer to that prayer. The prayer itself grew out of a slogan used in the early Church, a kind of snappy shorthand for what Catholicism is still supposed to be all about: "God became human so that humans might become divine."

Catholics believe that because Jesus shared our human life, we can share his. Because he became human, humans can aspire to the divine. Jesus showed not only the face of God, but the true face of the human person and thus the glorious place that men and women hold in God's creation. "The glory of God is the human person fully alive." That was another important slogan in the early Church, attributed first to St. Irenaeus, a bishop in late-second-century Lyons.

The saints embody what Irenaeus was talking about—the human person most fully alive, living the life that Jesus came to give, a divine life in human skin. If dogmas and doctrines are the theorem, the saints are the proofs of Catholicism.

The saints aren't angels. Nor are they like Hindu avatars—incarnate visitors from the Godhead. The saints are human, all too human in some cases. When the Church declares somebody a saint, she is not saying that the person never sinned or made a mistake. She doesn't mean that the saint said, did, or thought the saintly thing in every circumstance.

You can take the saint out of the world, but you can't take the world completely out of the saint. Saints can be as blinkered as the rest of us in their social and political opinions and as prone as others to the prejudices of their time and place. Sainthood doesn't even guarantee that these people were much fun to be around—some are known to have been quirky, cantankerous, and temperamental.

Saints, in short, are still sinners. But we don't have to go so far as to embrace Ambrose Bierce's cynical definition in *The Devil's Dictionary*: "A saint is a dead sinner, revised and edited."

What sets the saints—flaws and all—apart from the rest of us is their powerful thirst for the holy, for total communion with God. They stand out because of their constant struggle to rise above the selfish limits of their human nature, to love with all their strength, to live by the grace of God alone.

We don't know what secret sins or temptations Mother Teresa struggled with. Certainly her visible sins and failings were negligible. We suspect she may have confessed to a sin similar to the one Orwell guessed to be Gandhi's: "vanity . . . the consciousness of himself as a humble, naked old man, sitting on a praying mat and shaking empires by sheer spiritual power."

Mother Teresa did appear to be keenly aware of the persuasive moral power that lay in her stooped, diminutive appearance, her poverty, and her prayerfulness. And people were sometimes surprised at how little she suffered fools and how relentless and demanding she could be in pursuing her objectives.

Bob Geldof fronted a rock band called the Boomtown Rats and spearheaded celebrity concerts in the 1980s to raise money for Africa's needy. He met Mother Teresa in Ethiopia and came away with these thoughts:

The Love That Made Mother Teresa

There was nothing otherworldly or divine about her. The way she spoke to the journalists showed her to be as deft a manipulator of media as any high-powered American public relations expert. She does a sort of "Oh dear, I'm just a frail old lady" schtick . . . There was no false modesty about her and there was a certainty of purpose, which left her little patience. But she was totally selfless; every moment her aim seemed to be, how can I use this or that situation to help others?

Supposing this is an accurate description, is this mix of calculation, ambition, and media savvy inconsistent with holiness? Hardly. Did she, as Orwell wondered about Gandhi, compromise her religious beliefs by mucking around in the worlds of politics and media to achieve her objectives? Maybe a little. Does it disqualify her from sainthood? If you think so, you're laboring under a gingerbread, holy-card idea of sainthood. The mistake is to equate divinity and sanctity with otherworldliness—as if the truly holy don't need to have an action plan or to be briefed before meetings. As if the saint has somehow risen above the cares and realities of this world.

The saints of any day and age don't renounce the world so much as they put it in its proper perspective—as no lasting city but rather a place of pilgrimage and testing. Saints see earthly life as a passage on their way home to the Father. The saints may have their hearts in the heavenly highlands, but they always have both feet planted on this earth. This is why the saints have always been known to give until it hurts when it comes to helping relieve earthly sufferings and misery.

In Mother Teresa's case, media glare and attention were part of the cross she had to bear. But even this she transfigured with a perfect Catholic gesture: she would tell journalists that for every photo they snapped, she asked Jesus to please take a suffering soul out of purgatory.

What Becomes a Saint

"For me it is more difficult than bathing a leper," she said of meeting the press. But, she added, "the press makes people aware of the poor, and that is worth any sacrifice on my part." We have no good reason to doubt her sincerity in any of this. Why should a twentieth-century saint be above using political means and the mass media to spread the fragrance of divine compassion in the world?

It seemed, though, that people preferred to paint Mother Teresa on a stained-glass window, as a figure more ethereal than real. You had the feeling that people were trying to make themselves feel better, looking for ways to dismiss her witness, trying to get off the hook of living up to her example. Sometimes they would invoke her name as a kind of apologia for their own apathy: "What do you think I am? Some kind of Mother Teresa?"

But Mother Teresa couldn't be dismissed that easily. She still can't. People came away from her touched and moved. They couldn't quite describe it, but they knew they'd been in the presence of a holy woman. It wasn't only her reputation, some pious power of suggestion. People felt that way even when they didn't want to.

One day in Kolkata, she took a woman in off the street. The woman's body was a mess of open sores, infested with bugs. Mother Teresa patiently bathed her, cleaned and dressed her wounds. The whole time the woman never stopped shrieking at her with swear words, insults, and threats. Mother Teresa only smiled at her.

Finally, the woman snarled, "Sister, why are you doing this? Not everyone behaves like you. Who taught you?"

Mother Teresa said simply, "My God taught me." The woman asked to know her God. Mother Teresa kissed her on the forehead and replied, "You know my God. My God is called love."

3

When God Wants a Saint

Mother Teresa had about her what an older generation of Catholic writers termed "the odor of sanctity" — something like the sweet smell of spiritual success. This book is an effort to follow her scent, to track Mother Teresa down the trail she left behind. You are not about to read a systematic study, a critical biography, or an inquest. This is more a series of meditations on her life and her times, which happen to be the times we're still living in.

This book starts by taking seriously the Catholic assumption that saints aren't born and they aren't made. They're sent. Catholics don't believe that saints just spring up randomly, like wildflowers in the garden of a culture. They are not the products of their training, hard work, and perseverance, as a concert cellist or a golf pro might be. They are not beneficiaries of a special honor conferred by the pope or the Church.

The *Church* doesn't make saints. In fact, the Church's exhaustive saint-making procedures — combing over every word the candidate ever uttered in print or in conversation, interviewing all known associates and contacts, studying behavior, habits, and personality traits — are designed only to figure out whether *God* has made this person a saint.

Even after the person's cause is studied extensively, God still has the last word. The pope can't canonize or beatify anybody unless he can prove beyond the shadow of a doubt that the candidate is in heaven and has God's ear. The only way to prove this is to find a miracle, usually a cure or a healing, that can be chalked up to the saint's heavenly influence or intercession.

Mother Teresa would still be languishing in the "venerable" department of the Communion of Saints if it had not been proven that an Indian woman's huge stomach tumor vanished after the woman prayed for her help. That miracle enabled Mother Teresa to climb up the official ladder of sanctity from "Venerable" to "Blessed." But the Catholic Church requires two miracles before someone can reach the top and be called "Saint."

In Mother Teresa's case, the miracle that pulled her up that final rung was the cure of a Brazilian man. In 2008, the man was in a coma, dying from a malignant brain tumor in its end stages. While he was being prepped for a desperate, last-ditch surgery, his wife and their parish priest were praying for Mother Teresa's intercession. A half hour before he was scheduled to go under the knife, the man sat up, pain-free and fully awake. His doctors could find no explanation—his symptoms had disappeared.

This is where we get uncomfortable. We like to believe we're in charge, that we can find an earthly cause for every effect, a rational, scientific explanation for everything. But to understand the saints, we have to suspend our disbelief. It's part and parcel of the Catholic worldview to believe that history is *his* story, a divine work in progress, and that everything from your individual biography to the fate of nations is moving according to God's design and purpose.

According to the great Catholic spiritual masters, God "writes" the world the way human authors write a book. The big difference is that God can do more than just imagine scenes, plot, characters, and dialogue—he can create them. If God wants light, his word is his command: "Let there be light." If God wants the sea to split and Pharaoh's armies to be drowned, he makes it happen. If he wants a prophet, he goes to a vineyard and plucks up a farmer named Amos.

When God Wants a Saint

Now, that doesn't mean that Amos has to follow God—he is free to say no. The point is that God didn't stop calling men and women like Amos, didn't stop "writing" the world on the last page of the Bible. The Bible itself promises that God will keep adding chapters to the history of his Church until the end of time. Think of the saints as key players in God's narrative strategy. "It's all God's doing. When God wants a saint, he makes one," St. Thérèse of Lisieux wrote in her memoir.

Granted, in the making of saints, God seems to be repeating himself a lot. After all, Catholics believe that with Jesus, the Word made flesh, God told us everything we needed to know—about who he is, who we're meant to be, and how we're supposed to live.

If God has said what he had to say, why do we need the saints? The short answer is that we don't, necessarily. Jesus remains with the Church, as he promised—in the sacred Scriptures, in the sacraments, especially the Eucharist, and in the poor and dispossessed. That's all Catholics need to find true happiness in this life and salvation and bliss in the life to come.

So we're free to ignore the saints. We don't have to believe any alleged miracles; we can go a lifetime without praying for the saints' intercession before the throne of God. Nonetheless, the saints are another face of Jesus. In the saints, God keeps his conversation with humanity going, keeps his face ever before ours. The saints are God's answer to the question of what Jesus would do in a given time and place.

"In the life of a saint, we have a microcosm of the whole work of God," wrote Cardinal John Henry Newman, himself now a "blessed" on the holy rolls. In the saints, God reassures us of his love, shows us another way out, lights a path for us in the falling dark of the world.

4

God's Good News

Not all saints are created equal. Sainthood, as they say about politics, is all local. That's why you've never heard of the vast majority of those in *Butler's Lives of the Saints* or 99 percent of the nearly fourteen hundred saints named by St. John Paul II and Pope Francis in the last quarter of the twentieth century and the first quarter of the twenty-first.

Most saints are hometown heroes, local boys and girls made good — very good. That's not at all to diminish them. Every saint reflects the glory of Christ. But most were made saints because they were able to translate the gospel into a way of life that spoke in a special way to their time and place.

Some saints — a handful in the past two thousand or more years — are sent to bear a message that transcends their moment and culture. They're raised up at critical junctures in history, when great gospel truths are in danger of being hijacked by heretics or plowed under by Christian indifference and forgetfulness.

These saints function something like the chorus did in an ancient Greek play — giving us the divine Author's commentary on events as they unfold in the Church or on the world stage. These saints speak God's truth, in actions and in words, to the powers and principalities of their day. And in that they speak to believers of all ages.

Augustine was one of these rare saints. So were Francis of Assisi and Thérèse of Lisieux. There are many others, of course, many of them martyred for the message they were sent to deliver.

The Love That Made Mother Teresa

Mother Teresa of Kolkata will be numbered among these special saints. The good she did wasn't done in a vacuum; the prayers she prayed weren't prayed without context. In the chapters that follow, we'll see that through her life God cast a searching light on the world and the times we live in. Fine details of her life seem choreographed from above. Early episodes sound themes that are picked up later. Chance encounters become signs pointing to larger meanings.

Mother Teresa will be known as the first saint of the global village, of a world made smaller by money and media, travel and entertainment.

As the highways and waterways of the Roman empire paved the way for the Christian gospel to be preached to the ends of the known world, the communications networks of the information age brought Mother Teresa's face into every living room when that gospel had withered in influence, was fading from the collective memory of the West.

Unlike any other saint in history, in her lifetime she became known the world over, from mansions in the Hollywood hills to dirt hovels in El Salvador. That's because, unlike any saint before her, Mother Teresa was sent by God, not to her isolated nation or region, but to the whole world.

She was sent to help us see our globalized world as something of a false idol, a kind of mock mirror of Catholicism, history's first global religion — the word *catholic* meaning, of course, "whole" or "universal."

Catholics envision humanity — with all its different cultures, races, and even religions — as a single world family, a people loving one another and loving God. Mother Teresa showed us how far our world is from that. She showed us a world cleaved apart by blood and class, caste and creed, a world that fixed an impassable gulf between those who have too much and those who have nothing at all. She showed us a world in which people don't matter, especially the weak: the baby in the womb, the poor, the sick, the old. She showed us a world of people torn apart from within, not knowing who they are or what they should be about, not knowing what meaning there is to life, if any.

Mother Teresa became a household name in this world because God needed a witness, needed to send some sign that he is still on earth and that hope is growing like a seed beneath all the bleak contingencies of our days.

To carry out her task, she made herself transparent. We could see right through her—to Jesus. God made her to be the face of Christ in an age that couldn't remember what he looked like or why he came in the first place.

But she wanted us to see something more. She wanted to be our mirror. Whenever she fielded the inevitable question: "What's it like to be a living saint?" she always shot back, "I'm very happy if you can see Jesus in me, because I can see Jesus in you. But holiness is not just for a few people. It's for everyone, including you."

She came preaching universal holiness in a universally unholy time. Beneath all the messages she was sent to deliver, this was her most sublime: that God didn't share in our humanity so that a chosen few could be raised to the altars by the pope at St. Peter's. God has global ambitions. He wants to create a new humanity, a race of heroes and saints, a race that includes you and me.

Mother Teresa called for a revolution of saints, of holiness. What is holiness? Nothing but love as an all-consuming lifestyle. "Holiness," she said in both words and actions, "is the acceptance of God with a smile, at all times, anywhere, and everywhere."

Holiness is to give yourself to God, to give up all those things you don't need, all those things that don't lead you to God, and to spend your days serving your neighbors.

"Today, be the sunshine of God's love," she would say. "You are God's Good News; you are God's love in action . . . Each time people come into contact with us, they must become different and better people because of having met us. We must radiate God's love."

It was on the question of holiness that Orwell finally wrote off Gandhi and his approach to the world. "The essence of being human is that one *does not* seek perfection," Orwell argued. "Many people genuinely do not wish to be saints, and it is probable that some who achieve or aspire to sainthood never felt much temptation to be human beings."

As Orwell saw it, holiness was unnatural and inhuman; the would-be saint was a failed human being in flight from the responsibilities, attachments, friendships, and loves that make life worth living. What's more, he said, faith and holiness are "incompatible" with work for a better world. "One must choose between God and Man," he said.

Why spend time worrying about Orwell's opinion? Because he was his generation's most humane and eloquent spokesman for a humanism without religion—for the belief that men and women could live like brothers and sisters without believing they were children of the same God.

Also, most people, if forced to be candid, would have to admit that they share Orwell's suspicion about saints—Catholic, Hindu, or otherwise. We live in a culture that venerates great athletes and performers, that celebrates their years of training and self-denial in pursuit of bodily perfection, Olympic crowns, and other earthly garlands. But athleticism of the soul, any striving for self-mastery and perfection in the spiritual life, strikes most people as a little weird. Most of us would agree with Orwell: we don't want to be saints, and we're leery of people who do.

Orwell got it exactly right about so much in our troubled times. But Mother Teresa was sent to prove him, and the rest of us, dead wrong on this point.

In a life given to God in prayer and selfless love of the poor, she showed that it is possible to cast yourself into the arms of the living

God's Good News

God and still burn with the love of your neighbor. She shattered the myth that the holy person is unconcerned with the misery and suffering of this world.

Indeed, she said, the world will be saved only by saints, by people trying to become holy. There will be no peace in the world, or in any of our hearts, until we return to God and God's goals and ideals for human existence. "Only holiness," she said, "will be able to overcome all the sufferings and miseries of people and of our lives."

Mother Teresa was sent to teach us that holiness is our true human nature, the natural condition in which men and women are created. Holiness was not only possible, but desirable and necessary. We were made for holiness. She even gave us sound bites:

This is the perfect will of God for us: You must be holy. Holiness is the greatest gift that God can give us because for that reason he created us.

Sanctity is a simple duty for you and me. I have to be a saint in my way and you in yours.

Mother Teresa talked this way. She spoke the language of the Bible, made it sound so natural and ordinary. It wasn't anything new that she was sent to tell us. She reminded us that long before the followers of Jesus were called "Christians," they were simply called "saints." She said the same thing St. Paul used to say at the start of his letters: "You are called to be saints."

These weren't just words either. She made sainthood seem within our reach, a call to which we could respond. All we had to do was what she did—to give ourselves over to the mystery of God, to seek his will, not our own, to make every moment count. To do it all for Jesus.

What's so special about Mother Teresa is that she came to show us the glory that could be ours if we were fully alive. She came to give us another chance to see Jesus. Another chance to become truly human.

Part II

Love Like a Child's

There are many people who can do big things,
but there are very few people
who will do the small things.

Mother Teresa

5

The Hidden Life

This is one of the only stories we have from Mother Teresa's childhood:

One night she was sitting around the table after dinner with her brother and sister, swapping jokes, telling silly stories. Their mother sat with them for a bit, not saying much, then got up abruptly and left the room. The next thing they knew, every light in the house went dead. Mom had cut the power off.

"She told us that there was no use wasting electricity so that such foolishness could go on," Mother Teresa told a biographer with a hint of irony and wit. For her it was a light parable of origins, an explanation of her own no-nonsense style.

As episodes in the lives of the saints go, however, it's a disappointment. It certainly lacks the drama of St. Francis stripping bare in Assisi's town square to prove he doesn't need Daddy's money anymore. There is none of the pathos of St. Perpetua nursing her baby in a dank prison cell before being fed to the lions.

But with Mother Teresa, we don't have a lot to work with. Other saints who lived in the twentieth century—martyrs such as Maximilian Kolbe and Edith Stein, visionaries such as Padre Pio and Faustina Kowalska—give us tales of spiritual and moral combat, battles with the dark side of human nature and with the forces of evil.

With Mother Teresa we have pictures. Hundreds of them. Public posings, as if she were running for some spiritual office—laughing-eyed, holding babies; clasping the face of a dying, stick-figure man;

sharing a confidence with an anonymous low-caste constituent; half kneeling, half curled up on a gray chapel floor, chin in her chest, hands folded in prayer. She was the first saint whose story was told in coffee-table books.

People loved to take her picture as much as she loathed being photographed. They treated her like a living reliquary, focusing on pieces of her body: the wrinkled fingers like stuffed grape leaves working her rosary beads, the gnarled leathery feet, the face that looked as if it were chiseled from thousand-year-old oak roots.

Although she was an odd bird in the firmament of world celebrity—an old woman without money, a standing army, or sex appeal—she was easily among the most recognizable people of the century. Her face was so ubiquitous that it could get embarrassing. Can you imagine another saint having to fax a Nashville coffee shop and ask its proprietors to cease and desist from advertising that her wizened likeness had miraculously appeared in one of their sticky buns?

But if a picture tells a thousand words, it worked the opposite way with Mother Teresa. Even the ones in color seemed to come out black and white. Her eyes told us everything and nothing all at once. We all know what she looked like. We know next to nothing about how she got in the frame to begin with.

Although she lived in the age of satellite communications, the World Wide Web, and 24/7 cable news networks, she may as well have been ensconced behind medieval garden walls for all we know about her life, especially her beginnings.

With saints of centuries past, biographical black holes are understandable. They either wrote their own life stories, or their legends were passed on by devotees. In most cases, what we know is what these saints wanted us to know or what their posthumous handlers believed would be "edifying" for us to know.

That's why hagiography, as writing about the saints is known, all too often strikes us as all too pious and not quite real. This is not to say that what we read about the saints is a lie. It just means the wrinkles and warts get airbrushed out. What makes saints like the rest of us—their foibles and faults, struggles and failures, their true humanity, in other words—often gets left on the cutting-room floor.

What is baffling is that this brand of hagiography was permitted to persist in the case of Mother Teresa—a saint of the information age, a Nobel Prize winner who mingled with prime ministers and popes, the rich and the famous, who made powerful enemies both inside and outside the Catholic Church with her radical views on everything from abortion to war. You would think that every rock in the garden of her life would have been overturned, every room tossed, closets ransacked for skeletons, relatives and close associates shaken down for incriminating details.

People tried, of course. Fed up with the "drenching sycophantic publicity," British journalist Anne Sebba set off on a forensic fishing expedition, skulking around graveyards in Mother Teresa's hometown in Albania. Sebba came back with what she described as shocking findings: that Mother Teresa's late mother was fifteen years younger than her father and that Mother Teresa's older sister was born when her mother was just fifteen.

In her 1997 book, *Mother Teresa: Beyond the Image*, Sebba tried hard to pin the charge of "cover-up" on Mother Teresa—insinuating that she ordered the dates changed on her mother's and sister's gravestones so as "not to advertise to the world that [her] mother had conceived at such a tender age."

Sebba didn't have any evidence of a conspiracy, but that didn't really matter, because the charge itself was kind of silly. After all, in the early 1900s there was no shame in being a teenage bride and mother—it was common for families in that part of the world to marry off their young daughters in arranged marriages.

But that's how it always seemed to go with Mother Teresa. Even people who wanted to pillory her couldn't find any basic facts about her life. You'd read their exposés and come away knowing way more about their own hang-ups with the Catholic Church than you did about Mother Teresa.

The truth is we don't know much more about Mother Teresa of Kolkata than we do about those early virgin-martyrs who get a paragraph in *Butler's Lives of the Saints*.

Mother Teresa's authorized biographers seem forced to hurry through her formative years in a matter of a few uninformative pages. Dates don't add up or are kept vague. Sentences begin: "She was a born . . ." Fill in the blank with whatever you want: "leader," "missionary," "saint," and so on. It makes no difference; nobody can prove it anyway. Instead of character studies, we're forced to read stereotypes, such as this about her mother: "Drana was always busy, if not working in the home or helping others, she would be saying the Rosary." Invariably, at the end of a short chapter or two, you read a line such as: "The young Mother Teresa, who first felt a calling to the religious life at age twelve, entered the convent at eighteen."

The blame, to be fair, rests squarely with our subject. All of her biographers begin with a sort of disclaimer, as if to say that they tried but couldn't get close to her. "Over the years she had been consistently terse in her response to questions which endeavored to probe her personal life and motivation," Kathryn Spink apologizes in advance of her *Mother Teresa: A Complete Authorized Biography*.

Eileen Egan, a friend who traveled extensively with Mother Teresa, could do no better. Her 448-page biography, *Such a Vision of the Street*, is the best of the bunch. But even she devotes less than fifteen pages to the years before Mother Teresa became a nun, and much of that is taken up with background about Albanian Catholicism and politics. Her subject, she says, "was always reticent about details of her personal life."

But even supposedly independent journalists treated her with kid gloves, granting her an immunity from scrutiny scarcely conceivable for other public figures. Mother Teresa became a sort of godmother to Lady Diana, the Princess of Wales, and the two died in the same week in 1997. We could never imagine the press allowing Diana to get away with such generic, evasive answers as:

We were a very, very happy family.

No one thinks of the pen while reading a letter; they only want to know the mind of the person who wrote the letter. That's exactly what I am in God's hand—a little pencil.

Even the brilliant Malcolm Muggeridge, who exposed the brutality of Stalin's Russia and skewered with a gimlet eye politicians and cultural figures, was caught with his critical guard down. His *Something Beautiful for God* catapulted Mother Teresa to international fame and remains probably the finest interpretation of her life. But even he was reduced to making statements about her past that had no basis in the biographical record and could not possibly be verified. "As a child," he once wrote, "Mother Teresa was . . . already conscious that some special mission would be required of her, and preparing herself to undertake it."

The truth is that nobody really knows what she knew or when she knew it or how she became the person she became. That's part of her mystery, and a big part of her message for our times.

6

The Limits of Biography

Here is what we know: Mother Teresa was born Agnes Gonxha on August 26, 1910, in Skopje—in present-day Macedonia. She was the youngest of three children born to Nikola and Drana Bojaxhiu.

She was an Albanian Catholic, born in the year of the great Albanian uprising, and during her first years, her home city was invaded by Serbians who spent days on an ethnic tirade—raping, torturing, and murdering her neighbors and kin. Her official biographers are vague about the possible impact these events had on the family. "The Bojaxhiu family were very much caught up in this turmoil," writes one. "But as a family they were financially and lovingly secure."

Mother Teresa grew up initially in the comfort reserved for the prosperous bourgeoisie. Her father must have been a prominent figure—when he died all the shops and offices in the town closed for his funeral. He was a successful merchant and investor, served on the town council, and was often out of the country on business.

A generous man, especially with the poor and with the Church, Nikola's passion was Albanian independence. He hosted political strategy sessions in his home, was friends with legendary freedom fighters and patriots, and apparently helped bankroll the movement to establish an Albanian state in the Kosovo region. That's what apparently got him killed. At a political fundraising dinner in 1919, he was poisoned, presumably by angry Yugoslavian authorities.

The Love That Made Mother Teresa

The circumstances surrounding his death were chaotic and strange, and only one of Mother Teresa's biographers even reports them. Nikola came home from the fundraiser very ill. Drana, sensing he was dying, hurried young Agnes out the door to summon their priest to give Nikola the last rites. Agnes got to the church, but the priest didn't answer his door.

For some reason, Agnes then fled to the train station. There, standing on the platform, was a priest nobody had ever seen before. He rushed with her back to the house. The priest anointed Nikola with holy oil and prayed over him the prayers of the dying. Then he walked away into the night. Nobody got his name. They never saw him again. Nikola was dead by morning.

After Nikola's death, his business partners grabbed his share of everything and ran, leaving the Bojaxhius in financial straits. Drana took to supporting the family by sewing and rug making. Her children called her Nana Loke ("mother of my soul"). She was, by all accounts, a remarkable woman. In addition to becoming a successful entrepreneur, she went to Mass daily at the Church of the Sacred Heart down the street, brought food to the poor, opened the family dinner table to the homeless, and gave refuge to women in need. She would tell her children, "When you do good, do it quietly, as if you were tossing a pebble into the sea."

Mother Teresa, in the few remarks she made about her childhood, always mentioned her mother's hospitality.

> We had guests at table every day. At first I used to ask: "Who are they?" and Mother would answer: "Some are our relatives, but all of them are our people." When I was older, I realized that the strangers were poor people who had nothing and whom my mother was feeding.

For her part, Mother Teresa seems to have been a serious, bookish, and sort of sickly girl, prone to whooping cough and other infections. The name her parents called her, Gonxha, means "flower bud" in Albanian. Her brother, Lazar, said she was the kind of kid sister who wouldn't tell Mom when you stole from the cookie jar but still tried to make you feel remorseful about it. Young Gonxha loved music, played a pretty mean piano and mandolin, wrote some poetry, and acted in a few plays.

She was very active in church, singing in the choir and taking a leadership role in a young-ladies society devoted to the Virgin Mary. The parish priest, an energetic Jesuit named Fr. Franjo Jambrenkovic, encouraged the Rosary and other devotions. He started a library and made sure that Agnes and other young people read Catholic books, newspapers, and magazines. He preached often about the Church's missionaries, especially local priests serving in India.

With her mother, Agnes made yearly pilgrimages to the nearby mountain shrine of Our Lady of Cernagore in Letnice. On one of these occasions, perhaps on the day Catholics commemorate the Virgin Mary's Assumption into heaven, Agnes felt the first stirrings of her call to religious life while praying before a statue of the Virgin.

Mother Teresa said she began praying about what to do with her life when she was about twelve. "Sometimes I doubted that I had a vocation at all," she said. "But in the end I had the assurance that God really was calling me. Our Lady of Letnice helped me to understand this."

Attracted by what she had read of their work in India, she decided to join the Sisters of Our Lady of Loreto. Lazar, who by then was a lieutenant in the Albanian army, told her she was throwing her life away. She wasn't intimidated. "You think you are important because you are an officer serving a king of two million subjects," she replied. "But I am serving the King of the whole world! Which of us do you think is in the better place?"

When she told her mother, Nana Loke locked herself in her room and didn't come out for a day. When she emerged, she said to Agnes, "Put your hand in his . . . and walk all the way with him." Agnes set sail for India in late 1928 and never saw her mother again.

We know only slightly more about her adult life than we do about her childhood. Of course, we have her writings and public talks. And pictures, lots of pictures.

7

Not the "Big" Teresa

Mother Teresa insisted on living a private, interior life, even once she hit the big time. Especially after winning the Nobel Peace Prize in 1979, she could have been a real player in global affairs, with loads of moral capital to burn on issues she cared about deeply, such as AIDS, poverty, and abortion.

God, it would seem, delivered to her an international bully pulpit. But she refused to mount it. It is strange, when you think about it. In an overexposed, celebrity-obsessed culture, God raised up a world-famous saint who ducked the limelight and had no appetite for autobiography.

Since St. Augustine, who practically invented the genre, saints have filled libraries with their life stories. Mother Teresa left us no confessions, no journal of her soul. Her spiritual correspondence, such as it was, consisted of exhortative letters sent to her nuns, and one-line notes she scratched to supporters, things such as, "Let us do all for Jesus through Mary."

Did God miss an opportunity here? Wouldn't he have wanted his saint to broadcast her story to the world, to tell us how much she had in common with us, to hold herself up as a role model? Why didn't she tell us what she was like growing up, about the scars left by the tragic death of her dad? Or about her relationship with her mother and growing up in a single-parent home? Did she ever have a boyfriend? What demons did she wrestle with? Did she ever feel low-down and lonesome?

The Love That Made Mother Teresa

She gave us nothing, and we should wonder why. She lived in the very times we live in, and yet God sent her as a stranger just passing through, her life destined to remain a closed book. If you are inclined to think that God must have his reasons, you might say Mother Teresa's first miracle was living in this day and age and being able to fly beneath the radar, to preserve her zone of personal privacy.

Even the skeptic has to concede that a highly unlikely set of circumstances conspired to draw an iron curtain of hiddenness around her:

Would-be muckrakers stumbled in their own muck. Journalists who should have known better observed self-imposed gag orders. There were no whistle-blowers, no believable tales told out of school by disgruntled former coworkers. Even Communist thugs and tyrants seemed to have been called in on this job, to ensure that nobody could check her family history. By the time anybody knew who she was, the Communists had swept into power in Albania, establishing a totalitarian police state, making it impossible to interview friends and family or check records and dates. The forces of nature, too, behaved as if carrying out some unspoken mandate; when an earthquake leveled her childhood home and neighborhood in 1963, it was like a divine conversation stopper, God forever interring her past in rubble and ruin.

We are left without a clue. Except for one thing: her name. In an instance of self-disclosure so isolated and rare that we need to stand up and take notice, she made her official biographers duly report that she took the name of St. Thérèse of Lisieux and *not* St. Teresa of Avila. "Not the big St. Teresa but the little one," she said without volunteering or apparently being pressed for further explanation.

In the Bible, when God changes someone's name, it signals a change in that person's destiny. Abram becomes Abraham, the father in whom all nations will be blessed. Jacob becomes Israel, namesake for God's chosen people. Simon becomes Peter, the first pope, the solid rock of the Church.

It is the same in religious life. Often, when a woman becomes a nun, she leaves behind her birth name and takes the name of a saint. It's both a sign of her new God-given identity and a kind of declaration of intent to imitate that saint's virtues, to follow Christ in the particular manner that saint did.

So who was this Thérèse, beloved by Catholics as the Little Flower, and why did Agnes Bojaxhiu pick her to be her patron? We will never know about Mother Teresa's motives. She seldom quoted Thérèse or spoke about her.

But Thérèse's story is one of the great ironies in Catholic history. Little Thérèse was born near the end of a century in which the Christian civilization of the West seemed to be taking a dive, the century in which Nietzsche pronounced that God is dead and that Christians had killed him; the century when Darwin announced his "discovery" that man descended from apes; the century when the workers of the world were starting to unite around a revolutionary manifesto by Marx.

The saint God chose to raise up in this century was a bourgeois girl who entered a Carmelite convent at fifteen, was dead of tuberculosis ten years later, and never showed a whit of interest in the tumult shaking the world outside her cloister. She spent her days praying and doing the laundry, reading the Bible, and counseling novice nuns. She wrote some letters, a few plays and poems. She was known for her goodness, but accomplished so little that a fellow nun worried aloud that Thérèse would be hard to eulogize at her funeral: "She has certainly never done anything worth speaking of."

Thérèse was asked by her Mother Superior to write her life story, which she dutifully did, expressing in simple language her philosophy of life, which came to be called the Little Way. This Little Way meant living with a childlike sense of wonder at God's gifts, with a child's sense of dependence and trust. It meant, Thérèse said, finding the true divine significance "in the least action done out of love."

Published a year after her death, the book became a surprise best seller. It was translated into countless languages and catapulted Thérèse to the ranks of the most beloved and important saints ever. Canonizing her between the world wars, at a time of social unrest and uncertainty, Pope Pius XI declared that if everyone followed her Little Way, "the reformation of human society would be easily realized." A few years after that, Pope Pius XII called her "the greatest saint of modern times."

This was the saint Agnes chose as her patron. Not the "big" Teresa, the bold reformer and mystic who mapped the soul's interior mansions, landing herself in hot water with the Spanish Inquisition. Agnes chose the path of Thérèse the Little.

Born roughly a decade after Little Thérèse died, Mother Teresa took up the Carmelite's torch and bore her little light farther down the trail into the darkening recesses of the modern world, the world remade in the image of Nietzsche, Darwin, and Marx.

Daughter in spirit to Thérèse, Mother Teresa showed us that the world was not what we had made of it, that there was more to life than what the philosophers, scientists, and revolutionists told us. It was all so much simpler, so much lovelier.

Mother Teresa told us that we were children born, not of the chance survival of fitter ancestors or the determining struggle of economic classes, but of a God who willed and desired each one of us to be. We should live our lives like children of God, she said—trusting that our Father will provide, loving him with little acts of love, and loving all people as sisters and brothers.

She preached this gospel of childlike love in words and deeds that were uncomplicated and elegant, repeating them day in and day out, like water dripping on the stones of our uncomprehending hearts:

Not the "Big" Teresa

Jesus came into this world for one purpose: he came to give us the good news that God loves us, that God is love, that he loves you, and he loves me. He wants us to love one another as he loves each of us.

You and I have been created for greater things. We have not been created just to pass through this life without aim. And that greater aim is to love and be loved.

All is grace, Mother Teresa said, echoing Thérèse — God's love above us, God's love below us, God's love stretched all around us like the arms of Christ on the Cross. Love was her theory and her practice. She translated Thérèse's Little Way into a way of life that could be lived outside convent walls by anyone and everyone. A way of life by way of love.

"Live life beautifully," Mother Teresa told us. This is what attracted people to her. They could sense that she was trying to practice what she preached. They could see that she tried to make everything she did, even her smallest thoughts and tiniest gestures, an oblation, an offering of love. She would tell us all to do likewise: "Offer to God every word you say and every movement you make."

Mother Teresa believed that there is nothing so small that it can't be offered to God. The littler, the better. The smaller, the more beautiful. "There are many people who can do big things," she said, "but there are very few people who will do the small things."

Her life was made up of doing these small things: saying her prayers, going to Mass, washing clothes, cleaning the house, reading a letter to a blind man, holding the hand of a dying woman, changing the diaper of an AIDS baby. These weren't chores for her, but little gifts of herself, things she did for Jesus.

Everything we do, she said, from the time we rise in the morning until the time we lay ourselves down to sleep, can be done for the love of Jesus, can be offered as something beautiful for God.

The Love That Made Mother Teresa

The whole day can be a prayer, a dialogue with God. She asked, "Do you play well? Sleep well? Eat well? These are duties. Nothing is small for God."

In a century of "total war" and mass movements of violent social engineering, God sent us a saint who not only sweated the small stuff but told us that the road to heaven was paved with it. It was as if he had decided that the last thing we needed was one more great leap forward, one more manifesto for the creation of a new kind of man. God sent us a saint who preached a new kind of crusade, a little revolution of love.

She told us of a kingdom of love that enlarges its borders one touched heart at a time. In an age when so many had plunged the world into bloodshed trying to create heaven on earth, she showed us that heaven was already here, if only we had eyes to see it.

Mother Teresa of Kolkata was the saint of ordinary time, of the divine found in the routine. She reminded us that God comes to us not like a bolt out of the blue but in the din of the everyday, in our families and workplaces, in all the struggles and joys of our daily doings. Most of the time, though, we miss him because we never expect God to be so darn ordinary.

Mother Teresa knew we tended to have big ideas about meeting God, as if he was to be found only in dramatic, mettle-testing, high-noon-at-the-crossroads, down-on-our-knees moments. But she told us that God seeks us in the usual—in the people he puts in our path, in the trials and sufferings he sends our way.

Sometimes, she said, the greatest offering of love we can make to God is to hold our tongue or to smile. "Often just one word, one look, one action—and darkness fills the heart of the one we love," she would remind us.

Probably no other saint spoke or wrote as much about smiling as Mother Teresa did. For her, smiling was a medium for divine communication. A smile could heal, change lives, turn the world around.

Not the "Big" Teresa

A smile is the beginning of love.

Let us not use bombs and guns to overcome the world. Let us use love and compassion. Peace begins with a smile. Smile five times a day at someone you don't really want to smile at. Do it for peace.

What Mother Teresa said sounded so puny, so insignificant. Sometimes it could seem that she was just putting us on, seeing if we were really paying attention. But she was on to something. How hard it is to muster a smile when you feel hurt or snubbed, especially by somebody you love—a parent, a spouse, or a child. How your mood can be knocked down to curb level when you smile at somebody, and your smile isn't returned.

How could we expect peace among nations when we couldn't find it in our hearts to smile at a person who had offended us? It started to make sense, then, when she said, "We can never know how much good a simple smile can do."

Mother Teresa taught us that in the divine scheme of things, we can never know the significance of anything we do. But we don't have to, and we shouldn't worry about it. This was the big wet blanket she threw on our results-hungry world. Love as if you're sowing seeds, not expecting anything in return, was her message. It is not what we do, but how much love we put into what we do.

Could the parish priest in Mother Teresa's hometown ever have known that by simply doing his job—celebrating Mass reverently, hearing confession with patience and mercy, teaching kids to pray and care about the Church's mission—he was planting seeds, cultivating the sanctity of one of the century's great saints? And what of the anonymous editors and writers of those Catholic magazines Mother Teresa read as a girl; could they have known they were stirring a zeal for souls, inspiring a heart for the lowly, helping to make a saint?

The Love That Made Mother Teresa

In her gospel of childlike love, actions speak louder than words. But motives speak louder still. Everything depends on having the right intention. You can do really big things, she would say, but they won't mean a thing if you don't do them with love. "Unless the work is interwoven with love," she said, "it is useless."

8

By Way of Love

Karl Stern, the Catholic psychoanalyst, credited St. Thérèse of Lisieux with discovering what he called the Law of the Conservation of Charity.

This law, he explained in his great essay on the saint, states that "nothing which is directed either toward or away from God can ever be lost." Further, he said, "in the economy of the universe," there is an "inestimable preciousness . . . [in] every hidden movement of every soul."

In laymen's terms: God has so made the world that everything we do or don't do has cosmic significance. With each new moment, we are presented with a fundamental option — to direct our acts and intentions either toward God or away from him. To love or not to love. And our little decisions in these matters have spiritual consequences we can scarcely imagine. When we are mean, we increase the sum total of meanness in the world. When we are indifferent, the world's indifference to love spreads. But when we love, even in the littlest things, we fill the world that much more with the radiant fragrance of God.

This was the law of the universe that Mother Teresa was sent to explain. But hers was no new doctrine. It was as old as the Bible, which, along with the prayers of the Mass, seemed to be her sole font of inspiration and wisdom. She was only saying what St. Paul said: that we should pray without ceasing, that whatever we do, even if we're just eating or drinking, we should do it for the glory of God. Mother Teresa said only what Jesus had said: that unless we love like little children, we won't see the kingdom of God.

Mother Teresa wasn't a theologian or a Bible scholar. As is so often the case with the saints, however, she shined a new light on the Gospel, helping us see passages we had overlooked and connections we couldn't see before. Reading Scripture in her little light, we see how God always works through the lowly and the least likely — making his covenant with Abraham, a seventy-five-year-old herdsman; founding his kingdom on the shoulders of a shepherd boy named David; redeeming the world through a quiet virgin from Nazareth; building his Church on a team of ex–tax collectors and fishermen.

"God is truly humble," Mother Teresa marveled. "He comes down and uses instruments as weak and imperfect as we are. He deigns to work through us . . . to use you and me for his great work." She taught us to see what she called "the humility of God" — how he stoops down to our level, speaks to us in words we can understand, even goes so far as to become an infant in the womb, all to show us his love and to share his life with us.

She helped us to see the patterns of humility and littleness in the life of Christ, who, until his last three years, lived the same workaday life most of us live. "How strange that he should spend thirty years just doing nothing, wasting his time . . . he, a carpenter's son, doing just the humble work in a carpenter's shop for thirty years!"

Mother Teresa saw in the Eucharist a daily reminder and continuation of the Bible's story of God's humility, a living memorial of his example of love and self-sacrifice.

> When Jesus came into the world, he loved it so much that he gave his life for it. He wanted to satisfy our hunger for God. And what did he do? He made himself the Bread of Life. He became small, fragile, and defenseless for us. A bit of bread can be so small that even a baby can chew it, even a dying person can eat it.

By Way of Love

This was the good news she brought to a world hungry for God and hungry for love. We have to walk the path that Jesus walked, a path that begins in giving ourselves away. She told us that love begins where the self leaves off.

"You must first forget yourself, so that you can dedicate yourself to God and your neighbor." That's what she told Subshasini Das, who came to her in 1949 during the first days of Mother Teresa's ministry on the streets of Kolkata. A privileged Bengali girl, she presented herself to Mother Teresa decked out in jewels and a fine dress and saying she wanted to give her life to the poor.

Sent away with those cutting words, she returned after weeks of soul-searching shorn of her fineries and clad in a plain white robe. Subshasini went on to become the first nun in Mother Teresa's new religious order, the Missionaries of Charity.

You must first forget yourself. That was Mother Teresa's message for a narcissistic generation, to people self-occupied yet still strangers to themselves.

She watched patiently as wave after wave of young women and men shucked off their parents' Christianity and turned their hearts East, following some star they thought was rising, some new wisdom they thought would save them from the phoniness and soullessness of their consumer-material world. "People come to India," she would say, "because they believe that in India we have a lot of spirituality, and this they want to find . . . Many of them are completely lost."

Her idea of selflessness was the opposite of that preached by others in what Orwell called our "yogi-ridden age." The gurus and sages of the East preached liberation through negation, through a progressive detachment from all desires and passions until the person arrives at a spiritual state of egolessness, free from and indifferent to the cares of the world.

For Mother Teresa, detachment and self-denial were not the end goals of our striving. She said that we deny ourselves, struggle against our selfishness and fancies, in order to purify our vision, to give ourselves totally to God, and be joined to him in the most intimate embrace of love. We do not empty ourselves in order to be nothing, free of desire and need, but in order to be filled with divine life, to see and live with Jesus.

"Once we take our eyes away from ourselves—from our interests, from our own rights, privileges, ambitions—then we will become clear to see Jesus around us," she promised. One of those lost seekers who crossed her path was Morris "Mo" Siegel. In 1969, the summer of Woodstock, he launched an herbal tea company, Celestial Seasonings, Inc., that caught the first wave of the all-natural, organic health craze and rode it all the way to the bank. By 1985, he had sold his company for $40 million and was desperately seeking meaning, his midlife crisis manifesting itself in outfits with names such as Earth Wise and the Jesusonian Foundation.

He wound up, as so many of his generation did, in Kolkata, trying to find himself as a volunteer at Mother Teresa's home for the destitute dying. She poked him in the chest and sent him home with these words: "Grow where you're planted."

Mother Teresa knew it was easy to be selfless for strangers, to love people we don't know. So easy that it was no love at all. When it comes to love, she knew we are all big-picture people. We like love in the abstract—the poor, the sick, the handicapped—but we're afraid of close-ups, the flesh-and-blood poor people and sick people, the family members and friends whom God plants in our midst.

"It is easy to love the people far away," she would say. "It is not always easy to love those close to us. It is easier to give a cup of rice to relieve hunger than to relieve the loneliness and pain of someone unloved in our own home. Bring love into your home, for this is where our love for each other must start."

She sent us all home to learn how to love again. Long before anybody else had begun warning about the disintegration of the traditional family, Mother Teresa was telling us that our families were dying:

> The world today is upside down, and is suffering so much, because there is so very little love in the homes and in family life. We have not time for our children, we have not time for each other; there is not time to enjoy each other.

That was her diagnosis—God's diagnosis, if we believe she was a special rider carrying a message to our day and age. Mother Teresa judged the health of our civilization by our ability to smile or hold our tongues; by whether parents had time for their children, husbands for their wives, the young to listen to the stories of the old; by whether we knew how to laugh and play, to be tender, to be still, and to know that God lives in every person.

"Love starts at home and lasts at home . . . the home is each one's first field of loving, devotion, and service," she said. And from the bosom of the world's poorest families, she brought us tender stories of heroic love. She told us of the sacrifices made by leper parents, who must give up their newborns immediately upon birth or risk infecting them for life with the disease. She told us the story of one couple saying good-bye to their three-day-old baby:

> Each one looked at the little one, their hands going close to the child and then withdrawing, trying, wanting to kiss the child, and again falling back. I cannot forget the deep love of that father and mother for their little child. I took the child, and I could see the father and mother as I was walking. I held the child toward them, and they kept on looking until I disappeared from their eyes. The agony and pain it caused! . . . But because they loved the child more than they loved themselves, they gave it up.

She told us of the little girl she met in one of her schools in Kolkata. The girl had been hiding the free bread that the nuns gave students each day, and Mother Teresa wanted to know why. The girl told her that her mother was sick and there was nothing to eat in the house, so she was bringing the bread home to her. "That is real love," Mother Teresa said.

Real love is what she came to show us. The love of the little. A love that cracks the shell of all our self-delusion and flings open the doors of our hearts to Jesus. A love that takes as marching orders the words of John the Baptist: "I must decrease so that Jesus might increase."

Mother Teresa told us that we could be — in every moment of our lives — God's answer to somebody's prayers. We could be Jesus. If only we would let ourselves.

This is why we know so little about her, why she seems to have come to us with no childhood, no past — and why her biography seems to begin and end when she gives her life to Jesus. She wasn't trying to throw us off the trail or cover anything up. She was giving good directions to the lost.

We wanted her to talk about herself. But she was just trying to be a reflection. That's why whenever we asked about her, she pointed us to Jesus.

She knew that she wasn't the one we were looking for.

Part III

Our Calcutta of the Heart

The streets of Calcutta lead to every man's door,
and the very pain, the very ruin of our Calcutta of the heart
witness to the glory that once was and ought to be.

Mother Teresa

9

Behind the Walls

Mother Teresa's conversion to the poor came slowly.

From 1929, when she first landed in Kolkata, until the late 1940s, she lived and worked mostly within the insular confines of St. Mary's School, a prim-lawned, high-walled campus run by the Loreto Sisters. She spent her days teaching history and geography to girls lucky enough to have been born into colonial India's professional and political classes.

Had she wanted to, she could have looked beyond the walls and down upon one of Kolkata's worst *bustees*, as the slums are called. It was known as Motijhil or "Pearl Lake," an ironic reference to the foul pond in the center of the teeming maze of mud alleyways and shacks that were home to thousands of the poorest of the city's poor. For nearly eighteen years, she didn't even know the slum had a name. A group of girls from her school, led by its Jesuit chaplain, used to visit Motijhil every Sunday, bringing food and doing charitable works. Mother Teresa never went with them. In fact, during her years as a teacher and later, as principal of the school, she never said or did anything about the poor that anyone can remember.

Her biographers have a hard time accounting for these facts. In the short pages they spend on these years, they look for possible explanations. Her compassion for the poor was growing like a hidden seed, one suggests hopefully. She was the behind-the-scenes force urging her schoolgirls to minister in the slums, offers another.

The Love That Made Mother Teresa

Indulging the last refuge of a biographer with sketchy documentation, another tries a religious gloss: "The poor were always in her heart and on her mind. She did not speak about it because the Lord was calling her to do something else at that time . . . Her hour had not yet come."

She did have a few early encounters with the poor while training to be a nun. And these encounters are filled with prophetic import, heralding what she would one day become: "Mother of the world's poor."

For instance, while doing a brief stint as a nurse-aid in a rural Indian village, a man thrust his infant son, emaciated and blind, into her arms and demanded that the nuns take and raise the child or he would abandon him in the tall grass for the jackals to devour. In a diary-like account she contributed to *Catholic Missions* magazine in 1931, she described her reaction: "The poor child! Weak and blind — totally blind. With much pity and love I take the little one into my arms and fold him in my apron. The child has found a second mother. 'Who so receives a child, receives me,' said the divine Friend of all little ones."

Her few surviving writings from this time all read like this — a mix of pious uplift, cheery beneficence, and sentimental observation aimed to tug at the heartstrings. Listen to this dispatch from early 1935:

> When they saw me for the first time, the children wondered whether I was an evil spirit or a goddess. For them there was no middle way. Anyone who is good is adored like one of their gods; anyone who is ill-disposed is feared as though he were a demon, and kept at arm's length. . . .
>
> When I first saw where the children slept and ate, I was full of anguish. It is not possible to find worse poverty. And yet, they are happy. Blessed childhood! Though when we first met, they were not at all joyful. They began to leap and

sing only when I had put my hand on each dirty little head. From that day onwards they called me "Ma," which means "Mother." How little it takes to make simple souls happy! The mothers started bringing their children to me to bless. At first I was amazed at this request, but in the missions you have to be prepared for anything.

Even after we factor in these few early incidents, we see nothing in her early career that anticipates what was to come—a burning desire to serve Jesus in the poor, to strip herself of everything to share in their poverty, bring them to God, be their voice, and place their cause upon the conscience of the world. What emerges instead is a picture of a happy, accomplished young nun, a good organizational woman comfortably climbing the professional ranks of her religious order.

"I am a teacher, and I love the work," she wrote to her mother. "I am also head of the whole school, and everybody wishes me well here."

This note so distressed her mother that she rushed back a reply that began: "Dear child, do not forget that you went to India for the sake of the poor." Reminding her of the lessons of charity that she thought she had taught her, Nana Loke invoked the memory of a poor, alcoholic widow they used to visit and care for. "Do you remember our Filé?" she asked. "She was covered in sores, but what made her suffer much more was the knowledge that she was alone in the world . . . that she had been forgotten by her family."

Much later we would hear Mother Teresa using her mother's words to describe the world's poor. She would tell us that the greatest hunger is the hunger for love, the greatest poverty to feel unwanted. But for all those years she didn't touch the poor, didn't venture beyond the walls, never left the idyllic English-style gardens of St. Mary's.

The Love That Made Mother Teresa

The world outside seemed to be on fire—the last vestiges of the British Empire were convulsing and crumbling under the "soul force" of Gandhi's nonviolence. Millions had begun to swell Motijhil and the other slums of the imperial capital—refugees from religious violence, famine, and disasters both natural and political.

On August 16, 1946, the world crashed up against the walls of St. Mary's, and Mother Teresa could ignore it no longer. A "Direct Action Day" called by Muslim leaders sparked mob violence between Muslims and Hindus. Mother Teresa's compound was under virtual siege, and she was driven out in a dangerous, desperate search for food for the three hundred girls in her care. What she saw made her blood run cold: fires burning inside shattered storefronts; human remains splattered and dripping down from brick walls; bodies and parts of bodies strewn everywhere, on sidewalks, gutters, roads; vultures picking bones. Five thousand were killed that day, three times that number wounded.

Less than one month later, on September 10, 1946, Mother Teresa was riding the train from Kolkata to Darjeeling, on her way to make her annual retreat, when she heard a voice, speaking in her heart, as she later described it. It was Jesus telling her to quit the convent to live and work with the poor.

Her nuns still celebrate this date as "Inspiration Day"—the day God inspired her to start the work. During her lifetime, however, Mother Teresa ducked further inquiries about her special calling from Jesus. She would say only that she was sure it was Jesus and that his message was unmistakable. "It was an order. To fail it would have been to break the faith."

All we knew was that something dramatic must have happened. When she told people what she wanted to do, it came as a shock. It was so out of character that some of her friends worried. "We thought she was cracked," one priest confided to a biographer.

10

The Secret Visions

After Mother Teresa died, officials preparing her sainthood cause discovered a small cache of letters written to her spiritual directors and superiors during her early years. She had long ago destroyed her notes and diaries from this period and had asked others to dispose of letters she had sent to them. "I want the work to remain only his," she told them. "When the beginning will be known, people will think more of me, less of Jesus."

As if following some divine script, a few ignored her wishes. As a result, it is now possible for us to partially reconstruct the high spiritual drama of Mother Teresa's conversion to the poor.

In early 1947, four months after hearing the voice on the train, she wrote to Ferdinand Perier, a Jesuit who was archbishop of Kolkata. In this letter, she made her case for why he should allow her to undertake a new initiative among the poor, describing at length the voice she heard on the train and in the days and weeks that followed.

"I want Indian Missionary Sisters of Charity, who would be my fire of love amongst the very poor — the sick, the dying, the little street children," Jesus told her. "The poor I want you to bring to me and the sisters that would offer their lives as victims of my love would bring these souls to me. You are, I know, the most incapable person, weak and sinful, but just because you are that, I want to use you for my glory! Wilt thou refuse?"

She went on to describe how she disputed with the voice she heard, which came to her often while she was on her knees after receiving Holy Communion. She told him to go find somebody else, that she was frightened of the hardship and the ridicule she would have to endure. She promised to be a good nun if only he would let her stay put in her comfortable convent. But he kept cajoling her, challenging her with the refrain: "Wilt thou refuse to do this for me?"

Jesus told her that it hurt him deeply to see so many of the poor, especially poor children, lost to sin and Satan. "Draw them away from the hands of the evil one . . . There are convents with [a] number of nuns caring for the rich and able to do people, but for my very poor there is absolutely none. For them I long, them I love. Wilt thou refuse?"

Finally, she told the archbishop that Jesus had mentioned him specifically. Jesus wanted him to approve her request "in thanksgiving for the twenty-five years of grace I have given him"—a reference to the twenty-fifth anniversary of Perier's ordination as a bishop.

But the wheels of the ecclesiastical bureaucracy grind slowly, especially when somebody claims to be having conversations with Jesus. Throughout the year, Archbishop Perier prayed and consulted others about her request, trying to discern whether her "inspiration" was genuine. Mother Teresa kept writing to him, each note more urgent than the one before. "These desires to satiate the longing of Our Lord for souls, for the poor, for pure victims of his love, go on increasing with every Mass and Holy Communion," she implored.

In a letter dated December 3, 1947, she revealed that she had been granted mystical visions of Jesus and Mary. This is how she described the last of three visions she saw:

> [A] great crowd—they were covered in darkness yet I could see them. Our Lord on the Cross. Our Lady at a little distance from the Cross—and myself as a little child in front of her. Her left hand was on my left shoulder and her right

hand was holding my right arm. We were both facing the Cross. Our Lord said, "I have asked you. They have asked you and she, my mother, has asked you. Will you refuse to do this for me, to take care of them, to bring them to me?"

I answered, "You know, Jesus, I am ready to go at a moment's notice."

Archbishop Perier relented a month after receiving this last letter. By August, word came from Rome that Pope Pius XII had given her the okay to leave the Loreto Sisters but remain vowed to poverty, chastity, and obedience under the authority of Archbishop Perier. When Mother Teresa heard the news, she asked simply, "Father, can I go to the slums now?"

And go to the slums she did. On August 17, 1948, within a week of her thirty-eighth birthday, she walked out beyond the walls of St. Mary's wearing a plain white sari. She had five rupees in her pocket.

She took a short course in basic medicine, found a place to live in a convent of the Little Sisters of the Poor, and began her work. She started by teaching the alphabet to poor children in classes she conducted under a plum tree in the middle of the slum. Soon she was going from hovel to hovel, visiting the children's families, bringing them food and conversation.

One by one, former students joined her in the work. Together they attended Mass, prayed the Rosary, and cared for the old and the sick, the hungry and the dying. By 1950, this informal group of women was recognized by the Church as an official religious order, taking the name that, as we would later learn, Jesus had given her — the Missionaries of Charity.

11

The Christ We Pass By

Saints are always getting started by either discovering Christ in some mysterious poor person who crosses their path or deciding they must imitate Christ by selling off their worldly possessions and becoming poor themselves.

As Phyllis McGinley, the venerable Catholic poet and saint watcher, once wrote, "Just as regularly as folk tales begin, 'Once upon a time,' so half the biographies of saints start with, 'He first sold his estates and goods for the benefit of the poor.'"

Take the early instance of the Roman imperial soldier Martin. In A.D. 334, he gave half his cloak to a shivering, naked beggar he passed on the side of the road. Later, in a dream, he saw Christ wearing his half cloak and boasting to the angels of how Martin had given it to him. That's all it took to set him on the path to becoming St. Martin of Tours, one of the most venerated of all saints during the Middle Ages.

Mother Teresa of Kolkata will be remembered centuries from now as an ordinary nun personally touched by Jesus, called to abandon herself, to imitate his life in the slums, and to bring the good news of God's love to the poorest of the poor. "My little one, come, come, carry me into the holes of the poor . . . their dark, unhappy homes," he told her. "Come, be their victim. In your immolation, in your love for me, they will see me, know me, want me."

Jesus gave her a mission of charity: by their love she and her sisters would make his love known. By becoming poor, they would make the poor rich with the promises of divine life. Mother Teresa always told her sisters that in this mission, their own absolute poverty was as crucial as any work of mercy they performed for the poor.

Since the beginning, her Missionaries of Charity have owned only a sari, a pair of sandals, some undergarments, a crucifix they pinned on their habit, a rosary, a prayer book, an umbrella for monsoon season, a silver bucket for washing, and a thin bed. Despite the heat of the Indian summers, they didn't even allow themselves to own a fan. They drew no salaries, did no fund-raising, refused to accept government or Church monies for their programs. They lived day to day and hand to mouth, begging alms and food, just like the poor they served.

Beware of money and the desire for ease and comfort, for it will turn your heart from God, Mother Teresa taught them. "One loses touch with God when one takes hold of money. God preserve us. It is better to die," she would repeat. "Once the longing for money comes, the longing also comes for what money can give — superfluous things, nice rooms, luxuries at the table, more clothes and fans and so on. Our needs will increase, for one thing leads to another, and the result will be endless dissatisfaction."

Popes and archbishops, and other well-meaning folk were always trying to give her fine medical buildings, even old mansions in which to house her nuns and headquarter their work. Mother Teresa always said thanks but no thanks. "God save us from such convents where the poor would be afraid to enter lest their misery be a cause of shame to them," she would add.

Cardinal Terence Cooke of New York once offered to subsidize the work of her nuns in that city's slums. She smiled in reply. "Do you think, your eminence, that God is going to go bankrupt in New York?" Mother Teresa wanted to be a radical witness to the providence of God, to the reality that, as she put it, "God always provides."

And God always did provide. He never went bankrupt in New York or in any of the 123 countries where her mission spread. Until the end she was financed, not by Church or government agencies, but by individual contributions.

In lifestyle matters, the saints tend to read the Gospels literally. Mother Teresa was no exception. The saints read Jesus preaching, "You can't serve God and mammon [money]" and "Blessed are the poor," and they put themselves on the downward mobility track, becoming conspicuous for their lack of consumption of the things of this world. They read that the Son of Man had no place to lay his head, and they try to live as he did.

Like saints before her, Mother Teresa seemed sent to help us hear these strains of the Gospel, strains that grow harder to tune in to amid the noisy spoils and trappings of our daily lives. It's as if God knows that the more comfortable we become, the more we're tempted to smooth the edges off the hard sayings of Jesus, to pretend he was talking about somebody else, not us, and to treat the plain words of the Gospel as if he was just polishing a metaphor.

The saintly Dorothy Day, founder of the Catholic Worker movement and a friend of Mother Teresa, once wrote, "In all bad times of luxury and corruption in the Church, there was always a St. Francis, a St. Anthony, a St. Benedict, a Vincent de Paul, a Teresa and a Thérèse on the scene to enliven history."

Mother Teresa's times, at least on the surface, didn't seem all that corrupt or luxurious. It was, however, a very comfortable time in Church history, when millions of believers, especially in the West, were content to enjoy the fruits of their easy peace with mammon.

While many were supping at tables of relative plenty, Mother Teresa was kneeling outside our gates, showing us the great gulf fixed between us and the legions of Lazaruses begging for our scraps. While many of us were playing the part of the guy in the parable who passes by on the other side of the road, Mother Teresa was the Good Samaritan, binding the wounds of those our world beats up and leaves for dead.

She is most often compared to St. Francis, the rich boy who made himself poor and kissed the leper. But really she was more like St. Lawrence. He was roasted alive for impertinence in A.D. 258 because, when ordered by the emperor's men to turn over the Church's wealth, he showed up with a retinue of the destitute and smiled. "These are the treasure of the Church," he said.

Mother Teresa, too, wanted us to see in the poor the richness of Christ. "These are our treasures," she would tell visitors to her mission in Kolkata. "They are Jesus. Each one is Jesus in his distressing disguise." She taught us to meet our Maker in the poorest of the poor, to find our salvation there.

Christ in his distressing disguise. It had a strange, oracular ring to it—frightening, but compelling, too. Her patron, Thérèse of Lisieux, developed a deep devotion to the Holy Face—the image of the battered and bruised Lord crowned with thorns. For Mother Teresa, too, the face of the crucified Jesus could be seen in the poor. There was nothing symbolic or evocative about it. In the poor, she believed, we meet Jesus—not a reminder of Jesus, not a symbol of Jesus, but Jesus himself, face-to-face, hungering for our love, thirsting for our kindness, waiting to be clothed by our compassion:

> The shut-in, the unwanted, the unloved, the alcoholics, the dying destitutes, the abandoned and the lonely, the outcasts and untouchables, the leprosy sufferers—all those who are a burden to human society, who have lost all hope and faith in life, who have forgotten how to smile, who have lost the sensibility of the warm hand-touch of love and friendship—they look to us for comfort. If we turn our back on them, we turn it on Christ, and at the hour of our death we shall be judged if we have recognized Christ in them, and on what we have done for and to them.

The Christ We Pass By

In doing unto the poor as if they were Jesus himself, she was again only reading the Bible to us, repeating ancient Catholic wisdom. Everything she said repeated what Jesus said more bluntly at the end of the twenty-fifth chapter of the Gospel according to St. Matthew. Mother Teresa took his words on faith — that he would remain with us truly until the end of time, that he would come to us in the bread and wine we offer on the altar, and that when we look into the eyes of the hungry, the homeless, and the unwanted, we'll find his eyes looking back.

Catholicism has always been a religion of the God who hides his face in the faces of our neighbors, the God who discloses himself in humble things — a wafer of bread, a cup of wine, the poor. Catholics believe that by joining his divinity to our humanity and by becoming "true God and true man," Jesus has identified himself in some way with every human being born or yet to be born. In practical terms, this means that everyone you meet in some way bears to you the presence of Jesus, and vice versa.

Yet in the poor and in the Eucharist, we have a special presence of Jesus. In the Eucharist he gives his life to us, shows us his love. In the poor, he waits for us to give our lives to him, to show our love for him. As Mother Teresa explained it:

> Christ understood that we have a terrible hunger for God . . . that we have been created to be loved, and so he made himself a Bread of Life and he said, "Unless you eat my flesh and drink my blood, you cannot live, you cannot love, you cannot serve" . . .
>
> He also wants to give us the chance to put our love for him in living action. He makes himself the hungry one, not only for bread, but for love. He makes himself the naked one, not only for a piece of cloth but for that understanding love, that dignity, human dignity. He makes himself the homeless one, not only for the piece of a small room,

but for that deep sincere love for the other. And this is the Eucharist. This is Jesus, the Living Bread that he has come to break with you and me.

Throughout the centuries, saints have been sent to remind us of the miracle of the Eucharist and of the mystery of Jesus' presence in the poor. Rarely has the same saint been sent to remind us of both. But Mother Teresa seemed to sense that in our materialistic, consumer culture these truths had been disconnected, demoted to the stuff of symbol and poetry.

Kolkata, for Mother Teresa, wasn't only a city in India. Its teeming millions of poor and homeless, living in gutters and garbage dumps, became for her a symbol of the desolate slum of the modern heart. In an intriguing unfinished fragment, she wrote, "The streets of Calcutta lead to every man's door, and the very pain, the very ruin of *our Calcutta of the heart* witness to the glory that once was and ought to be."

In the ruins of our Calcutta of the heart, we could no longer see the glory that had been given to us like a divine gift — the gift of a God who comes to us in the poor and in bread and wine. "People don't know they have lost their faith," she said of us.

For her, our failure to see Christ in the beggar was a sign that we had lost our ability to find him in the Eucharist. We might think we believe these things, but we're wrong. We were playing out the mystery recorded in the Gospel — of Jesus coming into the world and not being recognized as God. "Today, as before, when Jesus comes amongst his own, his own don't know him," she said. "He comes in the rotting bodies of the poor . . . Jesus comes to you and me. And often, very often, we pass him by."

When Mother Teresa looked at the West, she didn't see power, progress, and prosperity. She saw a spreading poverty of the heart and spirit. We are smothered by our possessions, by our love of money and the things money can buy, she told us. We have too much, and yet we can't be satisfied. "There is hunger for more things," she said. "People need more cars, more machines."

In the mirror she held up to our age, we are so many camels straining through the eyes of a needle, serving mammon but not knowing it. We no longer have time to care for each other, for smiling, for touching, for serving God. She called us the poorest of the poor. "These people are not hungry in the physical sense but they are in another way," she said. "They know they need something more than money, yet they don't know what it is. What they are missing really is a living relationship with God."

This was her mission: to show us a living relationship with God. Although we didn't recognize it at the time, she was bringing us back, restoring the ancient understanding of Jesus—that our salvation is bound up in the mystery of his presence at the altar and in the poor.

In the beginning, the Eucharist was believed to create communion between God and each believer. At the same time it was supposed to create a culture of sharing between rich and poor. But in the Bible, we find evidence that faith in the Lord's presence in the poor was already sliding—that's one of the reasons we hear St. Paul and St. James denouncing the rich for profaning the Eucharist by their humiliation of the poor.

Early on, the saints railed against heretics who denied both the real presence of Christ in the Eucharist and in the poor. Like Mother Teresa, they could see that to lose faith in the one is to lose faith in the other.

St. Ignatius of Antioch, who was fed to the emperor's lions around A.D. 107, said, "Those who hold strange doctrine . . . have no regard for love, no care for the widow, the orphan, none for the orphan or the oppressed . . . because they do not confess that the Eucharist is the flesh of our Savior."

St. John Chrysostom, a few centuries later, put it this way: "Do you wish to honor the body of Christ? Do not ignore him when he is naked. Do not pay him homage in the temple clad in silk only then to neglect him outside where he suffers cold and naked-ness. He who said: 'This is my body' is the same one who said . . . 'Whatever you did to the least of my brothers you did also to me.'"

We find these same words on the lips of Mother Teresa in the late twentieth century. She wanted to teach us to "live the Mass"—to see the Eucharist as a sacrament of love and a sharing of lives, to find Jesus there in the radiant bread and wine and again in the streets of sorrow and suffering.

"Our lives are woven with Jesus in the Eucharist," she said. "In Holy Communion we have Christ under the appearance of bread; in our work we find him under the appearance of flesh and blood. It is the same Christ. 'I was hungry, I was naked, I was sick, I was homeless.'"

She showed us a way to live our days in unbroken contact with the Lord—in the living bread of the Mass and in the hunger of the poor. It wasn't that she expected us all to live as she lived. But she did insist, in a way that no saint before her had, that our salva-tion is bound up in some mysterious way with our love of the poor.

"The poor are the hope of mankind," she said. "They are also the hope of the people of America, for in them we see the hungry Christ looking up at us. Will we refuse him?"

We now know that her plaintive "Will we refuse him?" was the refrain that Jesus spoke to her during those fateful days of inspira-tion in 1946. She made his appeal her own. And through her, Jesus issued his call to our age.

At times it sounded as if she was giving us one last shot at salva-tion. The life we would be saving in serving the poor would be our own. In alleviating their material poverty we would find the cure for our spiritual poverty. In feeding their hunger, we would satisfy our own. In clothing their nakedness, binding their wounds, and listening to their stories, we would touch Christ and find the God for whom we are all looking.

12

You Can Love Only One at a Time

Mother Teresa restored the ancient Catholic ideal of almsgiving. Care for the poor, the widowed, the orphaned, the helpless, and the sick defined the identity and character of the early Church. Charity performed as personal service to God was what set Christians apart from the rest of the world.

The motives of the first Catholics were heavenly and divine as much as earthly and humanitarian. They wanted to anticipate on earth the kingdom that Jesus had told them would come. The hinge between these two worlds was the Body of Christ — in the poor and in the Eucharist.

Early devotional manuals instructed that the poor should be "revered as the altar" because, like the altar, they presented us with the body and blood of Christ. From the ordinary believer to the well-to-do, all were expected to set aside a generous portion of what they earned and owned to share with the poor.

But for many Catholics in Mother Teresa's day, almsgiving and charity had lost their savor. This would become a source of serious criticism and misunderstanding of Mother Teresa and her message.

The 1960s and 1970s were marked by what has been called "the irruption of the poor" into the conscience of the West. With the advent of rapid travel and mass communication, we could see for the first time the vast, worldwide scale of human want and misery.

The Scripture that Mother Teresa quoted the most — "Whatsoever you do to the least of my brothers, you do unto me" — became the basis for a thousand Church antipoverty action plans and initiatives. In the Third World, it became a battle cry for missionary priests, nuns, and theologians of liberation as they took sides and sometimes took up arms in the class war, seeking to liberate the ancient lowly, the wretched of the earth.

Mother Teresa was never radical enough, never angry enough for many in this crowd. For many, she stood for long-suffering charity and the church-of-the-status-quo, for "the poor you will always have with you." They stood for prophetic justice, for throwing the rich out to wail and gnash their teeth, for the kingdom come marching in on earth as it is in heaven—by the barrel of a gun, if necessary.

Invited to a United Nations conference in Vancouver in 1976 to discuss urban poverty and housing issues, Mother Teresa had to listen to the harangue of one panelist who accused her of letting the bourgeoisie "dump their guilt" by donating money instead of fighting injustice and changing the social system.

When her Missionaries of Charity started working in the slums of Lima, Peru, one of the world's poorest cities, a group of local priests published an open letter of protest. Instead of caring for the victims of a rotten global economic system, they cried, she should stand with them in working to overthrow it.

Until her last days, she endured the same criticisms—that she was putting a bandage on the cancer, that she was naive about the evils of neoimperialism and neocolonialism, that she was indifferent to the root causes of the exploitation and domination of the poor.

Her harshest critics, it often seemed, were people pulling down a decent wage as professional Catholic poverty-fighters. "Mother Teresa takes care of the poorest of the poor but never deals with why they are poor," a charities official for the British Catholic bishops complained to a newspaper the year before she died. In the same article, another British Church aid worker said: "We are fighting for justice . . . Mother Teresa limits herself to keeping people alive.

You Can Love Only One at a Time

She deals only with the disease [of poverty] and not with preventing it. But people in the West continue to give her money."

Her critics were right, of course—on their terms. She had nothing of substance to show for more than a half-century of work with the poor. The poor were poor and badly treated in Kolkata before she arrived. They are poor and badly treated still today. You could say the same for each of the countries where her nuns have set up shop.

Still, her critics' picture of her was a frustrating caricature. She did criticize the arms race in the Third World as a theft from the poor; she decried the avarice and greed by which some nations live high on the hog while others barely survive. She denounced new forms of imperialism and exploitation that she saw in the policies of rich nations forcing birth control, abortion, and sterilization on the poor. She made pointed appeals to world leaders on behalf of refugees and victims of war, and she was vocal against the death penalty, euthanasia, and abortion.

But she had no illusions that revolution or a change of political parties would improve the lot of the poor. She never faulted those working to change political institutions and economic structures nonviolently. She, however, heard a different calling. Mother Teresa worked from below, waged her war on poverty person to person, soul to soul. "I know there are thousands and thousands of poor, but I think of only one at a time," she explained. "Jesus was only one, and I take Jesus at his word. He has said, 'You did it to me.' . . . You can save only one at a time. We can only love one at a time."

Mother Teresa believed she was put here to bear witness to a sacred truth and to rescue that truth from denial or misunderstanding. She was here to tell the world—especially the poor—that God has a special love for every soul, that each of us is a child of God, endowed with deep dignity, worthy of the price paid in blood by God's only Son.

The Love That Made Mother Teresa

And she tried to love the poor the way Jesus loved the poor. "He didn't say love *the world*," she reminded us. "He said, love *one another*—right here, my brother, my neighbor, my husband, my wife, my child, the old ones."

The year before she died, she explained herself with a childlike parable:

> Once upon a time, a good man returned a fish to the water. People told him: "So what? You save one fish. Tomorrow the sea will drop hundreds onto the shore. What difference did you make?" The man answered: "For that single fish, I made all the difference in the world. I saved him."

Her critics were wrong when they accused Mother Teresa of ignoring the causes of poverty. It is just that her answers were biblical, not political.

For her, poverty wasn't a crime we could pin on the rich or the multinationals or the capitalist system. Not that she would have denied the existence of widespread, even systemic, injustices in the world. But she saw a more radical evil at work—human sinfulness. The world, as she showed it to us, was living out Jesus' parable of the Good Samaritan. "The greatest evil is the lack of love and charity, the terrible indifference toward one's neighbor who lives at the roadside assaulted by exploitation, corruption, poverty, and disease."

She came to start a revolution, a war of liberation. She came to set the modern heart free and heal its blindness, to help us see our God struggling alongside us, suffering in the poor.

She was visiting one of her missions in Brazil at the height of a bloody civil war between brutal military rulers and revolutionary guerillas supported by many Church workers and some Church leaders. A journalist asked where she stood. "My revolution," she said, "comes from God and is made by love."

For Mother Teresa, there could be no call more radical than the call she heard on that train to Darjeeling, the call heard by countless saints through the ages—to strip yourself of everything, to share in the poverty of the poor, and to live with them as brothers and sisters. This was the beginning of the heaven on earth that many in her day claimed to be fighting and killing for.

"To know the problem of poverty intellectually is not to understand it," was her gentle response to her critics. "It is not by reading, talking, walking in the slums and regretting the misery, that we get to understand it and discover what it has of bad and good. We have to dive into it, live it, share it."

That's what she and her nuns did. She defined poverty in terms so broad—demanding that love and charity and solidarity be extended to every area of human life—that she was far more radical than any of the revolutionaries of her day. Her revolution included reading books to the blind and the illiterate and helping them write letters to loved ones. Her sisters would visit the lonely, the sick, and the unwanted—just to talk and to let them know that somebody cares to listen, that God cares.

In her revolution, great victories could be won by words spoken in love, by the warmth of a hand extended in friendship. These were the kind of war stories she told us.

Once in London she was walking down the street and came upon a drunk man. She took him by the hand, looked into his eyes, and asked him how he was doing. His face lit up. "Oh, after so long I feel the warmth of a human hand," he said.

Another time in Kolkata she was telling a leper about the love of Jesus, how he became flesh and died to set us free to love. "Repeat that once more," he said to her. "It did me good. I have always heard that nobody loves us. It is wonderful to know that God loves us. Please say that again!"

Mother Teresa knew the poor as more than numbers or mouths to be fed. They were not simply members of some class of unfortunates. She knew the poor she served personally, and when she heard the cries of the poor, she heard them crying for more than bread.

The Love That Made Mother Teresa

Visiting one of her missionary outposts in Nezahualcóyotl, Mexico, a slum where people lived in huts of corrugated metal and plywood and breathed the foul stench of factory waste and diesel fumes, she asked the people what their greatest need was. One man spoke for the rest. *"La Palabra de Dios,"* he said simply — the Word of God.

In the cry of the disinherited and the oppressed, Mother Teresa could hear what many missionaries and social reformers in her day could not — the cry for God. Like her Lord, she knew that man can't live by bread alone. She would have agreed with St. Thomas Aquinas, that the hungry must be fed with bread before we preach the Word of God to them. But she was sent to remind us of the uncomfortable truth that the mission of Jesus was about far more than stamping out poverty and freeing men from earthly servitude.

Impatient for "results," many missionaries and other Catholics in her day had lost sight of this, reducing the gospel to a blunt means for raising the consciousness of the poor and stirring their outrage against injustice. It is interesting, now that we can read her private revelations from Jesus, that Jesus said nothing to her about social conditions or injustice — only about saving the souls of the poor from the Devil.

From the start, her Missionaries of Charity distinguished themselves by this passion for both the holiness and the salvation of the poor. "The poor are hungry for God," she told us. "They want to hear about Our Lord. They do not worry so much about material things; they want to hear that they have a Father in heaven who loves them."

Near the beginning of her work, Mother Teresa was stricken with a very high fever. In a delirious state, she felt transported to the gates of heaven, where she stood before St. Peter. He told her, "Go back. There are no slums in heaven!" Mother Teresa responded angrily, "Very well! Then I will fill heaven with slum people, and you will have slums then!"

You Can Love Only One at a Time

She wasn't preaching pie in the sky, a heavenly reward as the only answer to the woeful toilings of millions. On the way to filling heaven with the poor, she intended to change this world, too.

"When all recognize that our suffering neighbor is God himself, and when you draw the consequences from that fact, on that day, there will be no more poverty," she said. And again: "If everyone could see the image of God in his neighbor, do you think we should still need tanks and generals?"

13

War without Tanks and Generals

In a century of bloody revolution, when growing numbers in the Church were lured by the siren promises of violent class struggle, Mother Teresa was a sign of contradiction—a nonviolent warrior for reconciliation and communion.

Her refusal to point accusing fingers at ruthless dictators, corrupt politicians, and multinational corporate bandits scandalized many. That she would meet with them and sometimes accept donations from them was said to prove that she was nothing more than a chaplain to the rich, helping to salve their consciences and laundering their ill-gotten gains for them.

It is true that Mother Teresa's approach to the rich makes her something of a rarity in the history of the saints. To say that the rich have never been highly regarded by the saints is a bald understatement. In fact, many saints seem to have been sent specifically to reproach the Church for getting too cozy with the rich and powerful. But in our violent times, Mother Teresa was sent as a voice for peace, for an end to bloodshed and the rhetoric of hate.

Like saints before her, she sounded the alarms of Jesus—that riches can be dangerous and can turn a person's heart from God, that they can be shamefully gained or shamefully used, and that the rich are duty bound to share with the poor.

Like Jesus, the apostles, and the ancient saints, Mother Teresa told the rich—all of us in the West—that what we have doesn't really belong to us. "Richness," she said, "is given by God, and it is our duty to divide it with those less favored."

Always she pointed us back to the Eucharist, the table around which all man-made divisions are meant to vanish in the communion of divine love. "The beginning of Christianity is the giving," she said. "God so loved us that he gave his own Son. Jesus took bread, the simplest of foods, and he made that bread into his body. He made himself the Living Bread to satisfy our hunger for God."

She wanted us to see how radical Catholic charity could be, how the giving of alms in love could revolutionize relations between rich and poor — without violence, coercion, or hate.

Mother Teresa never said that everybody had to live the way she did. But she made it seem so beautiful and so liberating. She kept telling us that voluntary poverty — freely chosen and not imposed by accident or birth — was a glorious liberty. And she was most clearly a soul free from earthly thirsts, from the desire for money, or the things that money can buy. She had no attachments and lived without nest egg or safety net, as if she really was resting in the palm of God's hand.

Voluntary poverty such as that lived out by her and her nuns is a counsel — a prescription for living that the Church gives only to those seeking to live in perfect imitation of Jesus. But all of us, Mother Teresa said, are called to live with less in order to have more to give.

"Money is not enough, for money one can get," she would say. "The poor need our hands to serve them; they need our hearts to love them. The religion of Christ is love, the spreading of love." She wanted us to climb down from all our laps of luxury, to make many little sacrifices and to restrain our appetites, to become more and more detached from our possessions and creature comforts, to pare down and strip away everything we can do without.

Once a highborn Hindu woman approached Mother Teresa and said she wanted to help the poor. In the course of their conversation, she told Mother Teresa that she had a weakness for expensive saris. In fact, she said, the one she was wearing that day cost about 800 rupees. Mother Teresa's cost 8.

Recounting the story, Mother Teresa said she prayed silently to the Virgin Mary, seeking the right words with which to respond to the woman. Finally, she told her, "Next time, when you go to buy a sari, instead of buying a sari of 800 rupees, you buy a sari of 500 rupees, and with the remaining 300 you buy saris for the poor people."

Thus began one very wealthy woman's journey to the poor. Soon she was buying herself saris worth only 100 rupees and giving to the poor more and more of her money, time, and possessions.

These were the kind of success stories that Mother Teresa pointed to. If we had the ears to hear, we would have heard in these stories the slow but inevitable coming of the kingdom of God.

Like the story about the girl in the United States who asked that her parents not throw her a party or buy her gifts for her first Holy Communion. Instead, she wanted them to take all the money they would have spent and send it to Mother Teresa. Or the high-born Hindu couple who came to her with a huge sum of money, explaining that they had foregone the extravagances of a traditional wedding in order to give to her. "Mother, we love each other so much that we wanted to obtain a special blessing from God by making a sacrifice."

To critics, her stories seemed quaint but irrelevant in the face of the grinding poverty of Kolkata and the rest of the world. But she insisted that when the rich begin to make sacrifices for the poor, to deprive themselves of things they like and once thought they needed, something divine and earthshaking is going on.

"When a girl who belongs to a very old caste comes to place herself at the service of the outcasts, we are talking about a revolution," she explained. "The biggest one. The hardest one of all: the revolution of love."

The Love That Made Mother Teresa

For more than a half-century, Mother Teresa ran an international school of revolutionary love, using the poor as our teachers. "Only in heaven will we see how much we owe to the poor for helping us to love God better because of them."

One of the numerous free schools she set up all over Kolkata was born of a middle-class Bengali family's sacrifice and conversion to the poor. The man had been a refugee who never learned to read or write. He had risen from poverty to become an electrician and had raised four sons, with whom he ran a prosperous business. He had achieved what they call the "Indian dream"—a house inside a walled compound, where he lived with his four sons, their wives, and his ten grandchildren.

After hearing Mother Teresa speak one day, the man went home, talked things over with his family, and together they decided to open their compound during the day for use as a free school. Nearly three hundred students each day began passing through their gates to be educated by Mother Teresa's nuns.

In the early days of her work, Mother Teresa seemed to be thinking a lot about walls. In the few writings we have from this period, walls are a recurring image.

"Our work is outside," she told her first followers. "Outside the walls, where the other [religious] congregations do not go." Again, she warned, "We must not start institutions and stay inside. We must not stay behind walls."

Maybe she was thinking about the better part of twenty years she had spent behind the walls of St. Mary's, walls she perhaps saw as a symbol of her own isolation from the poor.

In a way, she was like some latter-day Joshua, marching patiently outside the walls we throw up around our hearts, showing us God in the poor.

She wanted each of us to experience our own "inspiration day"—to hear the voice she heard, to watch the walls around our Calcutta of the heart fall down flat.

Part IV

Mother in Our Dark Time

I have begun to love my darkness
for I believe now that it is a part, a very small part,
of Jesus' darkness and pain on the earth.

Mother Teresa

14

In a Time of Dying

Hers was a strange undertaking for a saint—some kind of a cross between a gravedigger and a candy striper in the terminal-cases ward.

Mother Teresa fed the hungry, gave comfort to lepers and the handicapped, and found loving homes for orphans. But the work she was best known for was caring for the destitute dying—the soon-to-be-dead who had nowhere else to turn. This work captured the world's imagination, drew a generation of pilgrims and postulants to her side in Kolkata, and eventually earned her the Nobel Prize.

Why did she bother? What was she hoping to accomplish? Sometimes it seemed as if she was trying to make up for a lifetime of the world's indifference by giving these people a clean, well-lighted place to die. Most of those she cared for were Hindus, and although her enemies whispered that she was doing death-bed baptisms, she wasn't trying to win souls for Jesus in any traditional missionary sense.

"Let the dead bury their dead." Hadn't Jesus counseled that? You would think there were more important things for a saint to be doing in her day. Surely, a world with as many problems as ours, a civilization this decadent, had need of a stronger remedy. But she was the one God sent us, and this was the task he gave her: to help the nobodies of the world go gently into that good night.

It proved to be a prophetic appointment. Kneeling by the bed-sides of the dying, she was granted a privileged window on our cruel times, times in which it seemed we had become a species bent on our own extinction: fathers sacrificing sons in wars of nationalism, ideology, and religion; mothers slaying babies in the womb; children abetting the suicides of their parents. From her vantage point she could see ours as a self-immolating generation bent on begetting none further, using drugs and devices, even going under the knife to keep from bringing newborns into the world.

Shutting the eyes of the dead in the charnel house of the twentieth century, Mother Teresa seemed to be trying to pry open the eyes of the living.

The story of how her ministry to the dying came about is by now well worn. In 1952, she was racing for shelter during a monsoon when she stumbled over a woman lying in a gutter. The woman's toes had been gnawed off by rats, and her body was crawling with bugs and worms, but she was still breathing. The diminutive Mother Teresa slung the woman over her shoulder and carried her to a nearby hospital. Hospital policy, she was informed, was to refuse admission to anybody who had no chance of surviving.

Mother Teresa put out again into the wind and rain, bearing the woman to another hospital, where she heard the same response. The woman died there. The next day Mother Teresa started demanding that government officials provide her with a place where she could help the poor die with dignity: "We cannot let a child of God die like an animal in the gutter."

With what we have learned since her death, we are able to see now that all this was no accident of biography. Reading those secret letters in which she records her interior visions and conversations with Jesus and Mary, we learn that Jesus was the one who wrote her job description. He told her, "I want Indian nuns, Missionaries of Charity who would be my fire of love amongst the poor, *the sick and the dying,* and the little children."

The disclosure of these visions, and the Church's raising her to the altars as a blessed, provides us with a kind of hagiographical hindsight, a new lens through which to look at the skeletal details that we've been given about Mother Teresa's life. We can now see that she was living out a vocation given to her before she was formed in her mother's womb, a divine consecration to be a prophet of life to nations in the thrall of a culture of death.

The biblical prophets were the mouthpieces of God. Their words, their deeds, and sometimes even their life circumstances were signs pointing to some deeper divine message. The prophet Hosea, for instance, found himself married to a serial adulteress whom he nonetheless loved with a tender mercy, striving to woo her back from her false lovers. His relationship with his wife was meant to dramatize God's undying love for his faithless "bride," Israel. In much the same way, we are invited to see a divine template, a deeper religious significance in events and experiences in the lives of the saints.

In Mother Teresa's case, even the stones of the local landscape seem to cry out, bearing witness to her calling in a dying world. One of the few descriptions we have of her hometown is this image, written by an American journalist passing through Skopje, then known as Uskiib, just a few years before she was born.

> Tombstones are always the prominent feature of a Turkish town, but Uskiib resembles an oasis in a desert of dead. Acres of them . . . a few erect but mostly toppling or fallen, surround the town and stretch long arms into it; they flank the main road and dot the side streets far out into the coun- try . . . The sight is gruesome, and one's mind is wont to picture the many massacres that have made this sea of silent slabs.

Mother Teresa was to be an apostle of life, a woman sent to show that all of us are children of one heavenly Father. How fitting that she be born on the outskirts of a vast burial ground for victims of fratricidal feuds and hatreds.

The Love That Made Mother Teresa

She was her age's most visible defender of the weak and the innocent. And again we find early signs foreshadowing her vocation. When Mother Teresa was two years old, she lived through a massacre of the innocents, as the Serbian army swept through Skopje raping young girls, impaling infants on bayonets, hanging men from trees, torturing hundreds, killing thousands. Ironically, it's an event that none of her official biographers mention. It took one of her sharpest critics, journalist Anne Sebba, to bring it to light, although she would find no divine significance in the event.

Mother Teresa said that she felt a love for souls begin growing inside her when she received her first Holy Communion at the age of five. A few short years later, she learned just what that love would require. Her father's assassination must be seen now in light of her later role as prophet against the false gods of religious nationalism. In watching her father die, wasn't she somehow being anointed in her own tears and those of her mother as they wept for a life sacrificed to these false gods?

A man of God was even placed on the scene to mark this grim rite of passage. We recall that mysterious priest, without name or background, who appeared out of nowhere to give her father the last rites before vanishing again into the night. Was he a messenger sent to signal to her, and to us, that to live out her vocation, Mother Teresa must first suffer in her flesh the mortal anguish of a world that refused to believe in the love of God and the brotherhood of man?

The God of the Bible works through the little and weak, the last ones you would expect. It was that way with Mother Teresa. Destined to become her age's most visible and beloved witness to the gospel of Jesus, she was born of a tiny Catholic minority in a region where Catholics were repressed and persecuted by Muslims and Orthodox Christians alike. She was later driven to a far-off land that was home to a bewildering array of ancient religions, beliefs, and customs. There, in the midst of religious traditions far more ancient than her own, she was given the seemingly impossible mission of proclaiming her God to be the one true God.

In sending her to Asia, God was placing her at the scene of one of the great failures of the Christian missionary effort, where, after twenty centuries of preaching, barely 1 percent of the people professed faith in Jesus. Yet she will forever be remembered as Mother Teresa of Kolkata, a Christian holy woman in the city named for Kali, a Hindu goddess who is perhaps the most well known of the manifold deities in the pantheon of Asian religions.

To start her home for the dying, Kolkata's city fathers gave Mother Teresa an abandoned building attached to one of Hinduism's most revered Kali shrines. No doubt they congratulated themselves on finding her an eminently practical location; the shrine was joined to Kalighat—a sort of perpetual municipal funeral pyre, where day and night the bodies of the dead are wrapped in white linen and consigned to the flames, to be reduced to ash and scattered in the Hooghly River that flows slowly into the sacred Ganges.

It was a good plan. The destitute could come to Mother Teresa's to die and could then be carted over to the crematory for the final disposition of their mortal remains. But given the symbolism that can be found in the events of her early life, we have to see more at work here than clever problem solving by urban planners. With scores of Hindu gods and goddesses, why did Mother Teresa's home for the dying wind up alongside a shrine to Kali? Why Kali and not, say, the piper god Krishna, or any of the many other Hindu or Indian deities?

Kali (literally, "the Black One") is revered as the giver of all life and the one who takes it all away. "Creatrix, Protectress and Destructress, that Thou art," a Hindu tantra exults. Another tantra portrays her this way:

> She stands in a boat floating upon an ocean of blood. The blood is the lifeblood of the world of children that she is

ever bringing forth, sustaining, and giving back. She stands there and sips the warm, intoxicating blood drink in a bowl made from a human skull that she lifts to her insatiable lips.

Idols of Kali are terrifying—black as soot, baring exaggerated breasts; eyes wild, tongue lolling, dripping with blood; wearing a necklace of freshly severed human heads, carrying a cleaver and a noose, posed in a feverish dance. Kali priests are said to have murdered the first Christian missionary, running the doubting apostle St. Thomas through with a spear in A.D. 72, after he called her cult "Devil worship." Yet well into the nineteenth century, Kali worship often continued to take the form of ritual orgies and human sacrifice.

By Mother Teresa's day, worship of the goddess had been largely domesticated. Thousands came to the shrine at Kalighat each day crying, "Mother! O Mother!" begging Kali for prosperity, a mate, children, and more. Kali priests still offered her blood sacrifices— no longer from strangled humans but from the slit throats of black goats.

Mother Teresa never said a word publicly about Kali or her cult, except for an enigmatic remark she made to Malcolm Muggeridge about her beginnings near Kalighat. "I was very happy to have that place for many reasons, especially knowing that it was a center of worship and devotion of the Hindus." It is obvious now that she saw profound symbolic significance in the site.

She named her new home *Nirmal Hriday* ("Place of the Immaculate Heart") in honor of Mary, the pure-hearted virgin who, by the power of God's Holy Spirit, became the Mother of Christ. It was a blunt contrast, to say the least: the image of the humble maiden Mary alongside the violent mother deity whose cult historically demanded child-sacrifice.

Was Mother Teresa lobbing an anti-ecumenical potshot at her Hindu neighbors, making a wry slur against their goddess? They probably thought so at first. In the early days of Nirmal Hriday, angry mobs, whipped up by the temple priests, staged protests and made death threats against Mother Teresa, accusing her of a stealth campaign to convert Hindus. That all ended when she took in and nursed one of her most virulent enemies, a young Kali priest who was dying of tuberculosis and had been denied care by the city's hospitals.

That was Mother Teresa's way, the way of love in the face of hatred. She loved Hindus and showed great respect for their beliefs and customs. But at the same time, she was animated by a deep love for Jesus and Mary. She was bearing witness to that love in dedicating her work to the Immaculate Heart. She no doubt also saw the hand of God at work. For from the sacred site where Hindus revered their mother-goddess, she would be able to show all the world the face of its true mother — the immaculate virgin who became the Mother of God, who was assumed into heaven and became the blessed mother of all nations and peoples.

Except for her bishop and perhaps Pope Pius XII, no one at the time knew that Mother Teresa claimed to have seen mystical visions of Mary and Jesus in 1946. So we could not appreciate until now the powerful symbolism she conveyed in the naming of Nirmal Hriday or why she opened its doors for the first time on August 22, 1952.

The date marked the tenth anniversary of Pius XII's consecration of the world to Mary's Immaculate Heart, an act of faith by which he implored Mary to intercede for the Church in her struggles against the atheist wave sweeping the earth in the form of Nazi and Soviet totalitarianism. Pius had been inspired by Mary's 1917 apparitions to three shepherd children in Fatima, Portugal. There the virgin warned of "wars, famines and persecutions" and said that Jesus wanted the world entrusted, or consecrated, to her maternal heart.

Now we can see the striking similarities between the Fatima apparitions and Mother Teresa's own private revelations — the apocalyptic images of a suffering world, the revelation that Mary is our heavenly mother, the urgent messages of salvation, the Rosary proffered as a spiritual weapon against evil.

At Fatima, the Virgin appeared to children. Mother Teresa was taken in a vision "as a little child" to stand beside Mary at the foot of the Cross of the suffering Jesus. The Fatima children were shown a vision of hell. Mother Teresa was shown what might be described as the hell of the living in a world without Jesus — "a great crowd . . . all kinds of people — very poor and children were there also . . . with great sorrow and suffering in their faces."

In one vision, she saw the people "covered in darkness," and in another their hands were lifted, reaching for her as they cried, "Come, come, save us. Bring us to Jesus." Kneeling next to her in the crowd, Mary gave Mother Teresa her mission: "They are mine. Bring them to Jesus. Carry Jesus to them. Teach them to say the Rosary, the family Rosary, and all will be well. Fear not. Jesus and I will be with you and your children."

Following in the footsteps of Mary, Mother Teresa was to become a sort of mother to the world, embracing all men and women as her children, showing them the way out of darkness and into the light. She was to become a mirror of the Immaculate Heart of her heavenly mother — like Mary carrying Jesus into the world, leading all people to the foot of his Cross.

As we will see, these visions defined her work and her outlook. It is not too much to say that Mother Teresa viewed the world as caught up in an apocalyptic struggle between the Immaculate Heart of Mother Mary and a dark, demonic perversion of motherhood at work in the world.

In the divine script written for her life, Mother Teresa of Kolkata was based alongside the cultic center of Kali to illuminate this clash of worldviews. She was not sent into the world to offer Catholic commentary on Hindu deities or devotions. Far more was at stake than any superficial concerns for religious tolerance and diversity.

In a Time of Dying

She was sent at a "post-Christian" moment in history, when Western societies were in the process of rejecting and moving beyond two thousand years of beliefs, values, and assumptions based on the teachings of Christ and the Church.

In the place of Christianity's one God, a multiplicity of deities had been raised up for veneration — from the gods and goddesses of ancient religions such as Hinduism, to the stranger conjurings of a new-fangled Druidry and Wicca. Planted in India, seat of the world's non-Christian religions, Mother Teresa showed us that in moving beyond Christianity, the world was actually sliding back into paganism — the shape of religion before revelation, before God chose to make his covenant with Abraham and to show us his face in Jesus.

Ancient pagan rites glorified and sought to control magically the forces of nature — the eternally recurring cycles of fertility, life, and death. Pagan worship included ritual sex along with ritual death in the form of child sacrifice and the killing of the weak.

Without ever using the word, Mother Teresa showed us the new paganism of our post-Christian world. In the West, the fervid orgies of the fertility cults had been replaced by an idolatrous glorification of sex. In place of ancient child sacrifices there was now a state-sanctioned cult of abortion and the "assisted suicide" of the weak.

None of this had anything to do with present-day Hinduism or the practice of any other world religion. Mother Teresa would insist that what is beautiful and true in Hinduism and other religions is what leads to love and fraternity. The new paganism she prophesied against was a sort of secular religion promoted by multinational corporations, rulers of nations, and international agencies.

But in the ancient images of Kali — of a mother who kills her young, a deity demanding human sacrifice — Mother Teresa found her central metaphor for the suicidal corruption of civilization in her day, for the dark cloud she saw covering the people in her vision.

15

Can a Mother Forget Her Child?

When she accepted the Nobel Peace Prize, Mother Teresa surprised even longtime supporters by devoting her speech to abortion, which she described as the "greatest destroyer of peace today."

Her colleagues had prepped her to talk about the nuclear arms race and neoimperialism in the Third World. The diplomats who had nominated her for the prize came expecting tales of uplift from her work among the poor and the dying. Instead she spoke from the heart about the Kaliesque — "a direct war, a direct killing — direct murder by the mother herself."

People never quite knew what to make of Mother Teresa's abhorrence of abortion and other forms of birth control. To many it seemed like a sentimental archaism, a kind of vestigial tic of her traditionalist Catholic piety.

And indeed her views were a throwback to the earliest days of Christianity.

Abortion, birth control, and infanticide were as old as the world, practiced in every culture and religion of the ancient East, and justified in the West by great philosophers such as Plato and Aristotle. Jesus entered the world from a mother's womb, took children in his arms, and said that his kingdom belonged to those who could become little children. And from the beginning, Catholics took their Savior's love for children and family life seriously. They saw abortion in the society around them as an abomination. In their oldest writings outside the Bible, they called it "child murder," said it was part of "the way of the Black One," one of their names for the Devil.

When she stood up and lectured the president of the United States about abortion during a prayer breakfast in 1994, Mother Teresa was saying something so old, it sounded new. She used almost the same words that a Catholic named Athenagoras used to rebuke the Roman emperor Marcus Aurelius in A.D. 175. Athenagoras said, "Abortion is murder . . . for the very fetus in the womb is a created being and therefore an object of God's care." Mother Teresa said, "The child is God's gift to the family. Each child is created in the special image and likeness of God for greater things — to love and to be loved."

By the late twentieth century, memories of Christian origins had long since faded. Abortion and birth control had come to be seen by world leaders, and many Christian leaders and ordinary believers, as humanitarian breakthroughs that promised to increase freedom for women and to make life easier for the world's poor by reducing the numbers of mouths to be fed.

Even many of Mother Teresa's fellow Catholics felt hers to be a strange fixation in an age with no shortage of atrocities and injustices to horrify the conscience. How, they wondered, could she single out abortion in a time of gulags and concentration camps, ethnic cleansing, suicide bombers, and world poverty?

She saw their indifference to abortion as a symptom of a culture under strong delusion, of a people whose hearts had become a valley of bones. It was laudable that so many Americans and Europeans were worried about children dying of starvation and disease in India, Africa, and elsewhere, she said. But why were so many of these same people unmoved by the plight of "the millions who are being killed by the deliberate decision of their own mothers" in their own countries? She knew the answer. "Abortion . . . brings people to such blindness."

For Mother Teresa, abortion was the mother of all issues, of every violence, and of all poverty. "Nations who destroy life by abortion and euthanasia are the poorest," she said. "For they have not got food for one more child, a home for one old person. So they must add one more cruel murder into this world."

If a mother is permitted to kill her baby, she said, everything must be permitted, every violence should be expected. "We must not be surprised when we hear of murders, of killings, of wars. If a mother can kill her own child, what is left but for us to kill each other?"

Many in her day, especially Catholic leaders, spoke heroically and eloquently against abortion, defending the rights of unborn children in the womb, warning of the corruption of democratic principles and medical ethics in countries that allow abortion. Mother Teresa's voice was unique in its starkness, dire and brutal in its honesty. She, more than any other figure in her time, insisted that we never speak about abortion without calling it what it really is. And to her, abortion was something demonic, Kaliesque—a mother who murders her child, who turns the womb into a tomb and the seedbed of humanity's future into a killing field.

"I do not want to talk about what should be legal or illegal," she said. "I do not think any human heart should dare to take life, or any human hand be raised to destroy life. Life is the life of God in us, even in an unborn child. And I think that the cry of these children who are killed before coming into the world must be heard by God."

Propaganda and mass media seemed to have broken down the last distinctions between truth and falsehood, good and evil. And Mother Teresa sensed, as George Orwell had before her, that our language had been debased and twisted "to make lies sound truthful and murder respectable," as Orwell put it in his essay on politics and the English language.

She never let us lie to ourselves, never let us make murder sound respectful. "You do not know what abortion has done and is doing to our people," she once wrote to India's prime minister. "There is so much immorality, so many broken homes, so much mental disturbance because of the murder of the innocent unborn child, in the conscience of the mother. You don't know how much evil is spread everywhere."

For Mother Teresa, abortion represented nothing less than the abolition of man, the denial of the God-given destiny of each human person. In putting enmity between mothers and their babies, abortion made the living the enemy of the not-yet-born, and the present the enemy of the future. By abortion, we who were created to be our brothers' and sisters' keepers had been transformed into their willing executioners.

Much like the first Catholics, she saw abortion — and its evil counterpart, euthanasia — as demonic and idolatrous. In her time, the unborn, the handicapped, and the elderly had become the human sacrifices demanded by a civilization that values only productivity and profits, that despises all who are too little, too sick, too broken, or too old to buy or sell or make things.

Against the false gods of her age, Mother Teresa told us what had been revealed to her — that Mary is our mother and we are her children, no matter who we are or what we believe. "Mother Mary is the hope of mankind," she said.

Once, a Hindu couple, married sixteen years but still childless, came to her door. They wanted her to pray for them, that they might conceive and bear a child. She promised them her prayers and told them that they should also pray this prayer together: "Mary, the Mother of Jesus, give us a baby." She prayed, and the couple prayed as she told them to. Within three months they returned to report that they were going to have a baby.

"You must have deep confidence in Mary," she told us. "She is the Mother of Jesus. She is our Mother . . . She loves you, and her Son loves you tenderly. Ask her again and again to be a mother to you." Mary was our mother and our hope because through her body, offered in love to God, Jesus entered the world. Mary made herself a vessel of true devotion, a temple for the living God, and by her love she enabled the love of God to be born in our midst.

Mother Teresa wanted us to contemplate with her this glorious mystery of the Catholic Faith—that God, the Creator of all that is, humbled himself to become a man and to prove his love for us. She wanted us to marvel, as she did, at how God spent nine months in a woman's womb, became a child, tiny and defenseless, suckling at a mother's breast, and growing up in a human family.

Out of her meditations grew her only genuinely original religious insight: that the Christian religion was a religion of divine childhood and holy family, of divine generation and new birth—and that this world religion began under the hearts of two expectant mothers.

Mother Teresa read deeply and spiritually into the biblical encounter of Mary, pregnant with Jesus, and her kinswoman Elizabeth, pregnant with John the Baptist—a moment Catholics remember as the Visitation, one of the five Joyful Mysteries of the Rosary.

For Mother Teresa, the Visitation unlocked the secret of Christianity. All the religions of the world begin with adults, with their search for God. Christianity, she showed us, begins with God's search for us, his coming among us as an infant in the womb.

> We read in Scripture that God loved the world so much that he gave his Son Jesus, who became small, helpless in the womb of his mother . . . And his mother, having the presence of Jesus himself in her womb—went in haste to serve others . . . to give him to others. And she went to serve her cousin who was also with child.
>
> And something very beautiful, something very wonderful happened at their meeting. The first one, first human being to recognize the presence of the coming of Jesus [was] . . . the little one in the womb of his mother [who] leaped with joy . . . It is so beautiful to think that God gave that little

unborn child the greatness of proclaiming the presence of Jesus on earth.

There was mystery and awe in her voice when she told us these things. An unborn child—John leaping in the womb of his mother, Elizabeth—was the first to proclaim the good news of God come among us. For Mother Teresa, the mother with child was at the heart of God's loving plan. In that dialogue in utero, in the loving meeting of two women with child, God revealed the infinite dignity of every human person, a dignity bestowed even before birth; he hallowed motherhood and childhood, the human family.

Mother Teresa taught us the "family Rosary," as she had been commanded in her private revelations from Mary. She showed us the Rosary as a family prayer of the children of God, as the story of God becoming a child in a human family so as to make every human family part of the family of God.

She repeated the ancient promises God made through the prophets: "Before I formed you in the womb, I knew you . . . You are mine . . . I have carved you in the palm of my hand. You are precious to me. I love you . . . Can a mother forget her infant, be without tenderness for the child of her womb? Even should she forget, I will never forget you."

She showed us our heavenly mother, and in that she showed us our Father in heaven. During a century in which the human person had been reduced to a beast of burden, fodder for war, and raw material for economic production, she showed us who we really are—special intentions, new creations, beloved sons and daughters. "Christ has created you because he wanted you," she said. "To him, each one of us is very special."

16

Brothers and Sisters All

Mother Teresa told us that we were all children of God, and that the Father desired a human family without borders on earth or in heaven, a family defined by love and the Spirit, not by flesh and blood.

All the world's bloodshed and violence she traced back to our failure to believe this simple truth. She warned, "If we have no peace, it is because we have forgotten that we belong to each other—that man, that woman, that child, is my brother or my sister."

In a generation marked by the irruption of rival gods, with believers of every stripe at each other's throats in religious warfare and sectarian terror, Mother Teresa showed deep respect for other religions without ever compromising her belief that in Jesus alone is found the way, the light, and the truth of human salvation.

She made herself a living example of the Catholic vision she wanted us all to see, the vision of a single universal family under the God revealed by Jesus. "By blood I am Albanian," she said. "By citizenship, an Indian. By faith, I am a Catholic nun. As to my calling, I belong to the world. As to my heart, I belong entirely to the Heart of Jesus."

She was a missionary in post-missionary times. Especially in Asia, the very idea of a Christian "mission" to save souls had fallen out of favor and been deemed dubious and backward, an affront to the consciences of Hindus and other non-Christians. In the name of tolerance and respect for other religions, many missionaries started teaching that Jesus was just another holy man, not the Son of God, and that believing in him wasn't the only way to salvation, but one of many valid paths in the modern spiritual wilderness.

Mother Teresa had too much respect for the truth of her own conscience to ever fall into this trap of denying her Lord or the mission of his Church. "I love all religions but I am in love with my own," she would say. "Naturally I would like to give the treasure I have to you, but I cannot. I can only pray for you to receive it."

She earned the trust and friendship of Hindus, Muslims, Buddhists, and atheists. Many called her "Mother" and came to her for prayers and advice. But everyone knew that her heart belonged to Jesus and that she hoped that their hearts would one day belong to him too. In this, she was a kind of missionary to missionaries, showing them new possibilities for preaching the gospel in an age of radical religious pluralism.

Her way was based not on learned dialogue but on personal witness and acts of love. "Proclaiming is not preaching—it is being," she said. "We must proclaim Christ by the way we talk, by the way we walk, the way we laugh—by our life—so that everyone will know that we belong to him." And watching her love in action—the way she talked, walked, and laughed—was perhaps the finest argument anyone could make for the joy and liberation that comes from believing in Jesus.

Making converts to Jesus, however, was not her focus. Rather, she tried to make converts to love. Only God can change a person's heart, she would say. Her job was to love—to radiate the love of Christ and, through her works of love, to show people God's love for them. By her love, she hoped to draw men and women near to God. From there, she said, it's up to God to take people the rest of the way.

"We bear witness to the love of God's presence," she said, "and if Catholics, Protestants, Buddhists, or agnostics become for this reason better men—simply better—we will be satisfied. Growing up in love they will be nearer to God and will find him in his goodness."

Mother Teresa was a missionary of reconciliation and communion, a healer of the hatreds that drive the human family apart and the sin that alienates us from God. She gave us a heavenly vision of the family of God—sisters and brothers of every race, religion, and class, worshipping the Father and serving one another, building a culture of thanksgiving and love. It sounded so beautiful, so right.

But few among us had ears to hear it. If her patron saint, Thérèse, lived in the days when God was declared dead, in Mother Teresa's lifetime they were still heaping the last spadefuls of dirt into his grave. With its death camps and obliteration bombings, gulags and genocides, the history of her century read for many like expert testimony that her God, if he ever really existed, was asleep at the switch or had recused himself from the affairs of his children.

Mother Teresa's God stood condemned in absentia before the tribunals of a shell-shocked generation. If he is a loving Father, as she claimed, why does he allow so many of his children to be born into poverty and deformity, to pass their days in sorrow and pain, to be slaughtered in senseless wars? If he is the true God, why do so many who claim to believe in him betray his teachings, cloaking their greed and ambition in the name of religion?

Mother Teresa's generation was the first to witness the rise of atheist regimes and political forces bent on "de-Christianizing" and even expunging the memory of belief from the human consciousness. It was also a time of deeply personal existential revolt, as many in anguish turned away from a God they felt had turned away from them and their world. Many more, lulled into indifference by the trappings of a consumeristic and materialistic culture, lived in a state of "practical atheism"—as if God didn't exist, as if there was only this life to live.

She was sent to an age often defined as one of "seeking," when the old answers of Christianity seemed to lead only to more questions.

The Love That Made Mother Teresa

Many who had not rejected religion sought new truths in the ancient wisdom traditions of India and the East. They found consolation in the teachings of Hinduism and Buddhism—that there's no such thing as a personal God, that life is a cosmic wheel on which the soul spins ceaselessly from birth to death to rebirth again, that what befalls us in this life is the result of our karma, of what we've done unto others in previous lives.

In this post-Christian landscape, God raised up Mother Teresa as a great mahatma, a teacher of wisdom from the East. She never debated theology or theodicy, never made an intellectual defense against atheist arguments or proposed to answer the problem of evil and innocent suffering.

To the anger and alienation, despair and doubt of our generation, she counterposed the Sign of the Cross. The sky is not empty and indifferent, she told us. The true God is such a personal God, and each soul is so dear to him, that he came down among us, exchanged his divinity to share in our humanity, to bear in our skin all the indignities and torments that could be heaped upon an innocent man—finally enduring the savage injustice of death by crucifixion.

"Jesus wanted to help us by sharing our life, our loneliness, our agony and death," she said to us. "All that he has taken upon himself and has carried it into the darkest night." We suffer nothing that he has not already suffered, endure no agony that he has not first endured. By entering into the blackness of our mortal anguish, Jesus has transfigured human suffering for all time, lashing our tribulations to his Cross, forever investing our dolor with divine meaning and purpose.

In some mysterious way, all the innocent suffering in the world has now been made a part of Jesus' sufferings for the salvation of the world. This was Mother Teresa's answer to those who were always asking her how God could allow children to perish in famines, earthquakes, and wars. "It is innocent suffering and that is the same as the suffering of Jesus," she would reply. "He suffered for us, and all innocent suffering is joined to his in the redemption. It is co-redemption. It is helping to save the world from worse things."

Those who suffer are not paying back some karmic debt incurred in a previous life. Nor are they victims of the negligence of an absentee deity. The innocent suffer for our failure to love and sacrifice, for our indifference. "If sometimes our poor people have to die of starvation," she told us, "it is not because God didn't care for them, but because you and I didn't give, were not instruments of love in the hands of God."

Only the Cross of Jesus makes sense of the senseless suffering in our midst. Without the cross, without a God who has suffered in our flesh, human suffering is only emptiness and absence, loneliness and meaninglessness. But joined to his Cross, no suffering is wasted if it is borne with love, with a desire to lessen the sufferings of others and to help in some small way to atone for the sins of the world. She told us:

> Pray thus when you find it hard: I wish to live in this world which is so far from God, which has turned so much from the light of Jesus, to help them—to take upon myself something of their suffering.

Mother Teresa taught each of her Missionaries of Charity to be a "witness of penance." They were to offer themselves for the sins of others, as Jesus did, to endure their sufferings on behalf of others, to suffer so that others would not have to. "We must be ready to take their place," she would tell her sisters, "to take their sins upon us and expiate them. We must be living holocausts." In the century of the Holocaust, she reminded us that we are meant to become "holocausts"—what St. Paul called living sacrifices of praise offered to God.

This is what Mother Teresa taught to a woman who came to seek her prayers for her ten-month-old daughter. The little one had been born with Down syndrome and was about to undergo risky heart surgery. Mother Teresa laid her hands on the child in prayer, then spoke these words to her mother: "God has given you this great gift of life. If God wants you to give it back to him, give it willingly, with love."

And people learned. In the loneliness and abandonment of their sufferings, they learned to surrender themselves to God and to give everything back to him with love, even their very lives. Mother Teresa was always telling us stories from her houses of the dying, of patients transfigured by the love they had been shown, made capable of offering heroic sacrifices of the spirit.

At an AIDS hospice she started in New York City, a young man motioned her to his bedside and whispered, "Mother . . . I get terrible pains, and I share my pain with the pain Jesus had in the crown of thorns . . . with the terrible pains Jesus had when they scourged him. And when I get pain in my hands, I share it with the pain of Jesus when he was crucified."

When that man was admitted, he had been bitter and angry. For twenty years he had been leading a dissolute life and had strayed far from the Church. The love he was shown at the hospice brought him to his knees and led him to confess his sins to a priest and hear the words of God's pardon. For the mercy he was shown, he wanted to spend his dying days offering sacrifices of pain and love for others.

Mother Teresa showed us a world being purified, ennobled by shared suffering in the light of the Cross. Early in her work, she even established a branch of the Missionaries of Charity made up of "suffering souls"—crippled, incurable, and severely handicapped persons who freely offered their sufferings in prayer for the sake of her mission, for Jesus' thirst for the salvation of souls.

She was a mother who did what she told her children to do. Mother Teresa rarely spoke of her loneliness for her own beloved mother, Drana. They had been so close, especially in the years of trial after her father died. And we can trace to Drana the spirit of love and the sense of Christ's immanence in the poor that became the hallmarks of Mother Teresa's work.

And yet they never saw each other again after young Gonxha left for the missions in India at age eighteen. Not long after, the Iron Curtain fell around her homeland; her mother and her people were forced to live for half a century under one of the history's most brutal dictatorships.

Mother Teresa and her mother wrote letters to each other. Throughout her life, Mother Teresa made futile diplomatic attempts to get her mother and sister out of the country. Her brother had been able to escape to Italy through his service in the military. She told many people that her greatest suffering was being separated for the rest of her life from her mother, who died in 1972.

But she also told her biographer Eileen Egan that for years the two had been offering up their sufferings for the salvation of souls. "You don't know what this sacrifice of not seeing my mother has obtained for my sisters . . . Her and my sacrifice will bring us closer to God."

17

Mother Teresa's Long Dark Night

For more than fifty years following her initial visions and locutions, Mother Teresa was wrapped in a dark, pitiless silence.

She only once more heard the voice of God, and she believed the doors of heaven had been closed and bolted against her. The more she longed for some sign of his presence, the more empty and desolate she became.

We always saw her smiling. She had a playful smile, mischievous, as if privy to some secret joke. Especially when she was around children, she beamed with delight. In private, she had a quick, self-deprecating sense of humor, and sometimes doubled over from laughing so hard. So many people who spent time with her came away saying that she was the most joyful person they had ever met.

Now we know that in secret her life was a living hell. As she confided to her spiritual director in 1957:

> In the darkness . . . Lord, my God, who am I that you should forsake me? The child of your love — and now become as the most hated one. The one — you have thrown away as unwanted — unloved. I call, I cling, I want, and there is no one to answer . . . Where I try to raise my thoughts to heaven, there is such convicting emptiness that those very thoughts return like sharp knives and hurt my very soul. Love — the word — it brings nothing. I am told God lives in me — and

yet the reality of darkness and coldness and emptiness is so great that nothing touches my soul.

Mother Teresa lived in a spiritual desert, panicked that God had rejected her, or worse, that he was there in the dark hiding from her. As if by some strange formula, the greater her success and public adulation, the more abandoned, humiliated, and desperate she felt.

There was a brief period, one month in 1958, when she was able to pierce the darkness. Her light came during a requiem Mass celebrated the day after the death of Pope Pius XII, the pope who had granted her permission to leave Loreto and go among the poor.

"There and then disappeared that long darkness, that pain of loss, of loneliness, of that strange suffering of ten years," she wrote. "Today my soul is filled with love, with joy untold, with an unbroken union of love." Four weeks later, the darkness had descended: "He is gone again, leaving me alone." She lived in this darkness until the end of her life.

Other saints have told of their spiritual torments and feelings of abandonment by God. In the sixteenth century, St. John of the Cross described the experience as "the dark night of the soul." But we would be hard-pressed to find another saint who suffered a darkness so thick or a night so long as Mother Teresa suffered.

John of the Cross and others wrote poems and spiritual canticles to describe their sufferings in God's absence and their frustrated longings for the embrace of his love. Mother Teresa never did. In fact, only her spiritual directors knew of her anguish. A few of her letters to them have been made public. And using lines drawn from these letters, we can piece together the stanzas of a sort of spiritual canticle depicting Mother Teresa's dark night of the soul:

I did not know that love could make one suffer so much . . .
of pain human but caused by the divine.

Mother Teresa's Long Dark Night

The more I want him, the less I am wanted.
I want to love him as he has not been loved,
and yet there is that separation, that terrible
    emptiness, that feeling of absence of God.

They say people in hell suffer eternal pain because
    of the loss of God . . .
In my soul I feel just this terrible pain of loss,
    of God not wanting me, of God not being God,
    of God not really existing.
That terrible longing keeps growing, and I feel as if
    something will break in me one day.
Heaven from every side is closed.

I feel like refusing God.

Pray for me
that I may not turn a Judas to Jesus
in this painful darkness.

Never before perhaps in the history of the saints have we been given such an honest and plainspoken account of the dark night of a soul.

In Mother Teresa's dark night, we can hear all the anguish of her century — the desolation of the poor, the cries of the unwanted children, of the atheist, of all those who can't murmur a prayer or feel to love anymore. It was as if in some way she was bearing their sufferings. And in this she seemed in some way to be sharing too in the sufferings of Christ.

"In you, today, he wants to relive his complete submission to his Father," she wrote in 1974 to a priest suffering his own spiritual blackness. "It does not matter what you feel, but what he feels in you . . . You and I must let him live in us and through us in the world."

We now see these words as beautifully autobiographical, reflecting her awareness that in her emptiness and poverty she was being mystically grafted onto the life of Christ—being emptied as he was in assuming our humanity and being crucified as he was in offering himself for our sins.

After her death, it was disclosed that in her early missionary days, long before hearing her call to the poor, Mother Teresa had quietly made a private vow of spiritual espousal—to be all for Jesus and to refuse him nothing.

From her letters, we can see that she understood her darkness as an ordeal, a divine trial. In the dark night, her vow of self-offering was being put to the test. Would she really refuse him nothing, drink the cup her Lord drank, lay down her life as he had laid down his life, offer herself as he did, completely and without reserve? In her dark night, Jesus was claiming Mother Teresa for his own, pledging himself to his spiritual bride, pruning away her self-love and pride, purifying her in heart, mind, and intention, stripping away all that would keep her from total union with him.

And again using lines from her private letters, we can compose the final stanzas of Mother Teresa's spiritual canticle, her response to her Lord and her dark night. These lines form a final prayer of self-oblation, an act of faith in which she makes herself a total gift—to share in Jesus' Passion and in his burning thirst for souls:

> For my meditation I am using the Passion of Jesus.
> I am afraid I make no meditation,
> but only look at Jesus suffer and keep repeating,
> Let me share with you this pain!
>
> If my pain and suffering, my darkness and separation,
> give you a drop of consolation, my own Jesus,
> do with me as you wish.
>
> I am your own.
>
> Imprint on my soul and life
> the suffering of your heart.

Mother Teresa's Long Dark Night

If my separation from you brings others to you . . .
I am willing with all my heart to suffer all that I suffer.
Your happiness is all that I want . . .

I have begun to love my darkness,
for I believe now that it is a part, a very small part,
of Jesus' darkness and pain on the earth.

I want to satiate your thirst

with every single drop of blood that you can find in me.
Please do not take the trouble to return soon.
I am ready to wait for you for all eternity.

Jesus came for her on September 5, 1997. She had been an apostle of joy and light in the dark final hours of the second Christian millennium.

She died almost one hundred years to the day after her patron Thérèse, the Little Flower of Lisieux. And their lives form spiritual brackets around the twentieth century. Thérèse, too, experienced a "night of nothingness" — on her deathbed, she heard demonic voices telling her that heaven was just a figment of her imagination.

Following Thérèse into this night of nothingness, Mother Teresa too sought the Holy Face of the Crucified in the crushed and the dying, walked the path of spiritual childhood in the small, ordinary realities of her days, and lived her life one little act of love at a time.

On the day Mother Teresa died, her sisters laid her in state beneath Our Lady of Fatima, a statue of the Blessed Mother depicted as she appeared to the children at Fatima. It was fitting in a way that no one could have known at the time.

Few knew that she had been guided all these years by apparitions and a voice heard one summer long ago. And few knew that she was trying to be a living expression of Mary's love for her children, to show us the blessed fruit of Mary's womb, Jesus. We can now see that Mother Teresa was among the firstfruits of the pope's consecration of the world to Mary's Immaculate Heart. The child called *Gonxha* "flower bud"—became the first bud of new Christian life, flowering from the century's bloody soil of wars, famines, and persecutions.

Mother Teresa had followed the call of the gospel and done all that had been asked of her by Jesus and Mary in those 1946 visions. They were visions for which her whole life had prepared her—and visions that she lived out for all generations to come. Kept secret during her lifetime, these things have been disclosed to us now in the early days of the new millennium so that we might understand more fully the meaning of Mother Teresa and the revolution of love that God was working in our midst.

She was our mother, coming to us in the dark night of our times to give us comfort and prove to us that we had not been orphaned by God. She taught us to call on our Father in all our desolations and diminishments, to cry out as she did—as children of his love, born of his desire, never out of his care, destined to love and be loved.

These were the lessons she was teaching every day in Nirmal Hriday. For the despised and unwanted, for those who had defiled themselves in sin and bad living, she wanted to prove the love of God, "to make the mercy of God very real and to induce the dying person to turn to God with filial confidence."

Helping others to die, she was teaching us how to live—with the confidence of children finding their way back to the loving arms of their Father.

She was an apostle sent to us in our time of dying, to a culture in which death had become the last refuge of the living. Hers was a ministry of final moments and last chances. She believed in death-bed conversions, that we were never too old to learn the lessons of spiritual childhood, that on this side of death it was never too late for any of us—or for the world.

"I am convinced," she said, "that even one moment is enough to ransom an entire miserable existence, an existence perhaps believed to be useless."

Mother Teresa's Long Dark Night

She once said, "All of us are but his instruments, who do our little bit and pass by." The little bit she did, she did with grace. But what she accomplished in her life was only partial. The accomplishments of the saints always are. They await their fulfillment in the lives of those who follow, in your life and in mine.

She turned our heads as she passed by, made us want to come and see what she saw, to follow where she was going.

Sources

Mother Teresa's collected writings would fill only a slender volume. Although there are many inspirational collections of her writings currently in print, and numerous others available from out-of-print booksellers, readers will notice that all of these collections draw from the same small pool of stories and reflections. The best single-volume collections of her writings are *Love: A Fruit Always in Season*, edited by Dorothy Hunt (Ignatius Press, 1987) and *Mother Teresa: Where There Is Love, There Is God*, edited by Father Brian Kolodiejchuk, M.C. (Image Books, 2010).

Except as noted below, quotations from Mother Teresa in this book have been drawn from the following biographies and collections of her writings:

By Mother Teresa

Love, A Fruit Always in Season. Edited by Dorothy Hunt. San Francisco: Ignatius Press, 1987.

The Joy in Loving. Edited by Jaya Chaliha and Edward Le Joly. New Delhi: Viking, 1996.

No Greater Love. Edited by Becky Benenate and Joseph Durepos. Novato, Calif.: New World Library, 1997.

Seeking the Heart of God, Mother Teresa and Brother Roger. San Francisco: HarperSanFrancisco, 1993.

Suffering into Joy. Edited by Eileen Egan and Kathleen Egan. Ann Arbor, Mich.: Servant Publications, 1994.

Blessed Are You. Edited by Eileen Egan and Kathleen Egan. San Francisco: Ignatius Press, 1999.

Biographies of Mother Teresa

Collopy, Michael. *Works of Love Are Works of Peace: Mother Teresa of Calcutta and the Missionaries of Charity*. San Francisco: Ignatius Press, 1996.

Egan, Eileen. *Such a Vision of the Street: Mother Teresa — the Spirit and the Work*. New York: Doubleday, 1985.

Kumar, Sunita. *Mother Teresa of Calcutta*. San Francisco: Ignatius Press, 1998.

Muggeridge, Malcolm. *Something Beautiful for God: Mother Teresa of Calcutta*. New York: Harper & Row, 1971.

Porter, David. *Mother Teresa, the Early Years*. Grand Rapids, Mich.: W. B. Eerdmans, 1986.

Raghu, Rai, and Navin Chawla. *Faith and Compassion: The Life and Work of Mother Teresa*. Rockport, Mass.: Element Books, 1996.

Royle, Roger, and Gary Woods. *Mother Teresa: A Life in Pictures*. San Francisco: HarperSanFrancisco, 1992.

Other quotations and sources not identified in the text are cited below:

1. A Mother Made Blessed
George Orwell's "Reflections on Gandhi" can be found in his *Essays* (New York: Knopf, 2002).

Sources

2. What Becomes a Saint

George Bernanos's quotation is taken from his "Sermon of an Agnostic on the Feast of St. Thérèse," in *The Heroic Face of Innocence* (Grand Rapids, Mich.: Eerdmans, 1999).

The quote from St. Irenaeus is from Mike Aquilina's *The Fathers of the Church* (Huntington, Ind.: Our Sunday Visitor, 1999).

Bob Geldof is quoted in Anne Sebba, *Mother Teresa: Beyond the Image* (New York: Doubleday, 1997).

3. When God Wants a Saint

Thérèse is quoted in David Scott, ed., *Praying in the Presence of Our Lord with Dorothy Day* (Huntington, Ind.: Our Sunday Visitor, 2002).

Cardinal Newman's quote is taken from Vincent Ferrer Blehl, ed., *The Essential Newman* (New York: New American Library, 1963).

4. God's Good News

George Orwell's quotes from "Reflections on Gandhi" can be found in his *Essays* (New York: Knopf, 2002).

For biblical examples of the first Christians being called "saints," see Acts 9:32; 26:10; Romans 1:7; Ephesians 1:1; Colossians 1:2; Philippians 1:1.

5. The Hidden Life

The quote from Malcolm Muggeridge is from his foreword to David Porter, *Mother Teresa: The Early Years* (Grand Rapids, Mich.: Wm. B. Eerdmans, 1986).

7. Not the "Big" Teresa

Quotes and background about Thérèse are drawn from James Wiseman, O.S.B., "The Spirituality of St. Thérèse of Lisieux as Seen in Her Poetry," and Peter Casarella, "Sisters Doing the Truth: Dorothy Day and St. Thérèse of Lisieux," in *Communio* (Fall 1997); John Sullivan, ed., *Experiencing St. Thérèse Today* (Washington, D.C.: ICS Publications, 1990); Barry Ulanov, *The Making of a*

Modern Saint: A Biographical Study of Thérèse of Lisieux (New York: Doubleday, 1966); Karl Stern, "St. Thérèse of Lisieux," in *Saints for Now*, ed. Clare Booth Luce (San Francisco: Ignatius Press, 1993); Conrad de Meester, O.C.D., *Saint Thérèse of Lisieux: Her Life, Times, and Teaching* (Washington, D.C.: ICS Publications, 1997); Pierre Descouvemont and Helmuth Nils Loose, *Thérèse and Lisieux* (Grand Rapids, Mich.: Eerdmans, 1996).

8. By Way of Love

Karl Stern's views are from "St. Thérèse of Lisieux," in *Saints for Now*, ed. Clare Booth Luce (San Francisco: Ignatius Press, 1993).

St. Paul talks about prayer without ceasing in Ephesians 6:18 and 1 Thessalonians 5:17. He talks about eating and drinking for the glory of God in 1 Corinthians 10:31. Jesus talks about being like children to enter the kingdom of God in Matthew 18:3.

The story of Morris "Mo" Siegel is told in "Putting the Red Zinger Back into Celestial," *Business Week* (November 4, 1991). Thanks to my friend and colleague Mike Aquilina for pointing this story out to me.

The John the Baptist quote is found in John 3:30.

9. Behind the Walls

Quotes and background from the early years of Mother Teresa's ministry can be found in David Porter, *Mother Teresa: The Early Years* (Grand Rapids, Mich.: Wm. B. Eerdmans, 1986).

10. The Secret Visions

Mother Teresa's letters are quoted in Missionary of Charity Father Brian Kolodiejchuk's "The Soul of Mother Teresa: Hidden Aspects of Her Interior Life," originally published by the Internet Catholic news agency Zenit, on November 28, November 29, and December 20, 2002. The articles are available in the archives at www.zenit.org. These letters are now published in Brian Kolodiejchuk, ed. *Mother Teresa: Come Be My Light* (New York: Image, 2009).

Sources

11. The Christ We Pass By

Phyllis McGinley is quoted from her book *Saint-Watching* (New York: Viking Press, 1969).

For Jesus on God and mammon, see Matthew 6:24 and Luke 16:9–13. He pronounced blessings on the poor in Matthew 5:3 and Luke 6:20. He claimed to have no place to lay his head in Matthew 8:20 and Luke 9:58.

Dorothy Day is quoted in David Scott, ed., *Praying in the Presence of Our Lord with Dorothy Day* (Huntington, Ind.: Our Sunday Visitor, 2002).

The quote from St. Lawrence is from Lawrence Joseph, "The Communion of Saints," in A *Tremor of Bliss: Contemporary Writers on the Saints*, ed. Paul Elie (New York: Riverhead, 1994).

Jesus promised to remain with us until the end of time in Matthew 28:20; to come in bread and wine in Matthew 26:26–27, Mark 14:22–23, and Luke 22:19–20; and to be present in the poor in Matthew 25:31–46.

The quotes from St. Ignatius of Antioch and St. John Chrysostom are from Mike Aquilina's *The Fathers of the Church* (Huntington, Ind.: Our Sunday Visitor, 1999).

12. You Can Love Only One at a Time

For the early Church's reverence of the poor "as the altar," see Mike Aquilina's *The Mass of the Early Christians* (Huntington, Ind.: Our Sunday Visitor, 2001).

For Mother Teresa's "favorite Scripture," see Matthew 25:40, 45.

The British charities officials are quoted in the *Guardian* (October 14, 1996). Also reported in Antonio Gaspari, "A Saint in Action," *Inside the Vatican* (December 1996).

Thomas Aquinas says, "A man in hunger is to be fed rather than instructed" in discussing "almsdeeds" in his *Summa Theologica*, II-II, Q. 32, art. 3.

14. In a Time of Dying

The American journalist passing through Skopje is quoted in Anne Sebba, *Mother Teresa: Beyond the Image* (New York: Doubleday, 1997).

Quotes and background on Kali are drawn from David Kinsley, *The Sword and the Flute* (Berkeley: University of California Press, 1975) and Rachel Fell McDermott and Jeffrey Kripal, eds., *Encountering Kali* (Berkeley: University of California, 2003).

Mother Teresa's remarks about Kalighat are found in Malcolm Muggeridge, *Something Beautiful for God* (New York: Harper & Row, 1975).

15. Can a Mother Forget Her Child?

Quotes and background on Kali are drawn from David Kinsley, *The Sword and the Flute* (Berkeley: University of California, 1975) and Rachel Fell McDermott and Jeffrey Kripal, eds., *Encountering Kali* (Berkeley: University of California, 2003).

For the condemnation of abortion in the oldest Christian writing outside the Bible, see the *Epistle of Barnabas* and the *Didache* in Maxwell Staniforth, trans., *Early Christian Writings* (New York: Penguin, 1968). On these points, see also, Michael Gorman, *Abortion and the Early Church: Christian, Jewish, and Pagan Attitudes in the Greco-Roman World* (Downers Grove, Ill.: InterVarsity Press, 1982); John Riddle, *Contraception and Abortion from the Ancient World to the Renaissance* (Cambridge, Mass.: Harvard University, 1992); and Martin Bergman, *In the Shadow of Moloch: The Sacrifice of Children and Its Impact on Western Religions* (New York: Columbia University, 1992).

Athenagoras is quoted in Rodney Stark, *The Rise of Christianity* (Princeton, N.J.: Princeton University, 1996).

The mystery of the Visitation can be found in Luke 1:39–56.

Mother Teresa quotes rather freely from the following biblical texts: Psalm 139:13; Jeremiah 1:5; Isaiah 43:1, 4; 49:15–16.

Sources

16. Brothers and Sisters All

St. Paul speaks of offering our lives as living sacrifices in Romans 12:1.

17. Mother Teresa's Long Dark Night

All quotations from Mother Teresa's unpublished letters to her spiritual directors, including the lines used to compose her "spiritual canticle," are taken from J. Neuner, S.J., "Mother Teresa's Charism," and Albert Huart, S.J., "Mother Teresa: Joy in the Night," in *Review for Religious* (September/October 2001). These letters can also be found in Brian Kolodiejchuk, ed., *Mother Teresa: Come Be My Light* (New York: Image, 2009).

About the Author

David Scott is a Los Angeles–based scholar, writer, and editor with a special interest in religion and culture. In a career that spans three decades, he has published hundreds of articles in journals and periodicals in the United States and abroad.

His essays and reporting have appeared in the Vatican newspaper, *L'Osservatore Romano,* as well as in *National Review, Commonweal, Crisis, Inside the Vatican, National Catholic Register, U.S. Catholic,* Godspy, Beliefnet, Catholic News Service, and elsewhere.

Scott's books include: *The Catholic Passion: Rediscovering the Power and Beauty of the Faith* (2005); *Praying in the Presence of the Lord with Dorothy Day* (2002), and *Weapons of the Spirit: The Selected Writings of Father John Hugo* (1997), co-written with Mike Aquilina.

Scott has held the top editorial positions at the nation's largest independent Catholic newspaper, *Our Sunday Visitor* (1993–2000), and the world's largest independent Catholic wire service, Catholic News Agency (2010–2012).

Currently he serves as Vice Chancellor for Communications for the Archbishop of Los Angeles. He lives in Los Angeles with his wife, Sarah, and their five children. More of his work can be found at www.DavidScottWritings.com.

Sophia Institute

Sophia Institute is a nonprofit institution that seeks to nurture the spiritual, moral, and cultural life of souls and to spread the Gospel of Christ in conformity with the authentic teachings of the Roman Catholic Church.

Sophia Institute Press fulfills this mission by offering translations, reprints, and new publications that afford readers a rich source of the enduring wisdom of mankind.

Sophia Institute also operates two popular online Catholic resources: CrisisMagazine.com and CatholicExchange.com.

Crisis Magazine provides insightful cultural analysis that arms readers with the arguments necessary for navigating the ideological and theological minefields of the day. *Catholic Exchange* provides world news from a Catholic perspective as well as daily devotionals and articles that will help you to grow in holiness and live a life consistent with the teachings of the Church.

In 2013, Sophia Institute launched Sophia Institute for Teachers to renew and rebuild Catholic culture through service to Catholic education. With the goal of nurturing the spiritual, moral, and cultural life of souls, and an abiding respect for the role and work of teachers, we strive to provide materials and programs that are at once enlightening to the mind and ennobling to the heart; faithful and complete, as well as useful and practical.

Sophia Institute gratefully recognizes the Solidarity Association for preserving and encouraging the growth of our apostolate over the course of many years. Without their generous and timely support, this book would not be in your hands.

www.SophiaInstitute.com
www.CatholicExchange.com
www.CrisisMagazine.com
www.SophiaInstituteforTeachers.org

Sophia Institute Press® is a registered trademark of Sophia Institute. Sophia Institute is a tax-exempt institution as defined by the Internal Revenue Code, Section 501(c)(3). Tax I.D. 22-2548708.